# ARIANA GRANDE

# ARIANA GRANDE

Her Life and Music, Era by Era

## GEORGE GRIFFITHS

SEVEN DIALS

First published in Great Britain in 2025 by Seven Dials,
an imprint of The Orion Publishing Group Ltd
Carmelite House, 50 Victoria Embankment
London EC4Y 0DZ

An Hachette UK Company

The authorised representative in the EEA is Hachette Ireland,
8 Castlecourt Centre, Dublin 15, D15 XTP3,
Ireland (email: info@hbgi.ie)

1 3 5 7 9 10 8 6 4 2

Copyright © George Griffiths 2025

The moral right of George Griffiths to be identified as
the author of this work has been asserted in accordance
with the Copyright, Designs and Patents Act of 1988.

All rights reserved. No part of this publication may be
reproduced, stored in a retrieval system, or transmitted
in any form or by any means, electronic, mechanical,
photocopying, recording, or otherwise, without the
prior permission of both the copyright owner and the
above publisher of this book.

A CIP catalogue record for this book is
available from the British Library.

ISBN (Hardback) 978 1 3987 2849 3
ISBN (Export Trade Paperback) 978 1 3987 2850 9
ISBN (Ebook) 978 1 3987 2852 3
ISBN (Audio) 978 1 3987 2853 0

Typeset by Input Data Services Ltd, Bridgwater, Somerset

Printed in Great Britain by Elcograf S.p.A.

www.orionbooks.co.uk

*I'm so into this book, I can barely breathe.*
Ariana Grande, hopefully (if she ever reads this)

# CONTENTS

*Introduction*   1

Chapter 1: Career Beginnings and *Victorious*   7

Chapter 2: *Yours Truly* and the Beginnings of a Pop Career   20

Chapter 3: *My Everything* and the Journey to 'It Girl' Status   37

Chapter 4: *Dangerous Woman* – A Career-shifting Statement   64

Chapter 5: The Manchester Bombing and *Sweetener*   89

Chapter 6: *Thank U, Next* and the Magic of the Imperial Phase   115

Chapter 7: *Positions*, Marriage and 'Rain On Me'   146

Chapter 8: Slowing Down, Divorce and *Eternal Sunshine*   167

Chapter 9: Transition into Acting, *Wicked* and Oscar Nomination   189

Chapter 10: *Eternal Sunshine Deluxe: Brighter Days Ahead, Wicked: For Good* and What's Next?                    212

*Acknowledgements*                    229
*Image Credits*                       231
*Notes*                               233

# Introduction

Ariana Grande may be small in stature (five foot one inch, to be exact) but she stands tall – monolithic, in fact – over most of her peers in modern pop music. Not least because of her signature platform stiletto boots and high ponytail . . .

Many perhaps wouldn't have guessed that the girl with dyed red hair with a secondary role on a Nickelodeon sitcom was a future superstar, but now Ariana Grande is someone who, in a way, seems to have *always* been famous.

In the pantheon of modern pop superstars, you can slot her in as a child of Britney Spears and Mariah Carey, see her as benefitting from the rise of Lady Gaga, Katy Perry and Rihanna, plus count her as a peer of Taylor Swift, Miley Cyrus and Selena Gomez. She's also helped to influence the new generation of pop stars; from Billie Eilish and Chappell Roan to Sabrina Carpenter, who seems to be the most emulative of Grande at the peak of her commercial powers, yet with a touch more irony and physical comedy.

But one thing Ariana Grande has that most of her

peers don't? That voice. *The* voice. Four octaves, to be precise, with a whistle register to rival even the Queen of Melisma, Mariah Carey herself. Instantly recognisable regardless of her timbre or key, whether she's belting out a swoony mid-tempo ballad or using it to spit bars over hip-hop inspired beats. Ariana's voice is a once-in-a-generation calling card and it's helped her transform from a children's TV actress to a debutante pop girlie in the making, to a dominant force in pop music (someone who has very much helped shape the culture of what releasing new music can look like in 2025, but more on that later) and, in her latest and most surprising role yet: Oscar-nominated actress.

But who *is* Ariana Grande? And what does her music say about her?

Ariana Grande-Butera was born to Joan Grande, CEO of a marine communications company, and Edward Butera, owner of a graphic design company, in Boca Raton, Florida, on 26 June 1993 (which, fact fans, makes her a Cancer). She has one older half-brother, Frankie, and is of Italian descent. The name 'Grande' has been pronounced *gran-day* for most of her career, but according to Ariana herself when talking to Beats 1, her maternal grandfather, Frank Grande Sr, pronounced it *gran-dee*. The more typical day pronunciation was, she says, popularised in her childhood by her half-brother Frank 'Frankie' Grande Jr and it's the pronunciation that stuck when she became famous.

Grande Sr – who died during the promo cycle for

Grande's second album *My Everything* in July 2014, was one of her biggest inspirations. Grande said to Beats 1 that it was in honour of her late grandfather that she still performs under the moniker Ariana Grande to this day (although in her 2024 film debut in *Wicked*, she was credited for the first time as Ariana Grande-Butera in a nod to her roots on the Broadway stage).

Fame is a game that must be played. Sometimes you win and sometimes you lose. Grande's ascent to a supernova-sized talent was one such gamble and it's paid off in dividends in 2025. The term 'big pop girl' is overused nowadays, but in her case it really does apply.

Across her now-seven studio albums – including two Christmas EPs and a live album, *k bye for now (SWT live)* and the soundtrack to *Wicked: Part One* – Ariana Grande has always worked best when pushing against the expectations of what she *should* do as a mainstream pop act.

Ariana's debut album, *Yours Truly*, was reworked into an ode to vintage pop and R&B, before a sacrifice to the pop gods was made on the much more electronic *My Everything*, while *Dangerous Woman* saw her mature-up her image, just as she switched up her release schedule so the hyper-personal breakup album, *Thank U, Next*, followed on less than a year from the experimental *Sweetener*; a breakaway from the long-established release schedule of A-list pop acts, it had reverberations that are still felt (and emulated) to this day.

In the latter part of her pop career, Grande has truly

taken ownership of her art. Sixth album *Positions* was a surprising return to the R&B roots of her debut album, while her most recent release, *Eternal Sunshine* was the long-awaited divorce album, spiked with heady electronica and references to Robyn and Britney Spears. Not, then, your typical record about divorce, babe, divorce! (Sorry, Adele!)

Grande's music operates on a higher plane when it reflects, and often comments on, her personal life. This is why *Sweetener* and *Thank U, Next* are often referenced by critics and fans alike as her best works. Songs like 'No Tears Left to Cry', 'Thank U, Next' and even the disco-drenched Lady Gaga collaboration, 'Rain On Me', don't just work on a basic level as next-level bangers – which, let's be clear, they absolutely are – but as a commentary on Ariana's own lived experiences, lending them an enviable level of depth not afforded to most standard Top 40 fare. When she discusses the impact of her trauma, washed away by a storm, on 'Rain On Me', that statement comes from a woman whose biggest traumas have been front-and-centre of most media headlines. To work through them and come out the other side alone is an amazing achievement, to have made tangible *art* along the way is nothing short of extraordinary.

Since releasing her first material as a pop star in 2011, part of the thrill of following Ariana Grande's journey as an artist is seeing where her sound will go next. 'The Way' featuring Mac Miller was filled with the bounce and verve of early Mariah Carey records, while her switch-up into straight pop saw her mixing around with spiky EDM (Electronic Dance Music) on 'Break Free' with Zedd and even lovelorn synth-pop in the sensual 'Love Me Harder' with fellow future superstar The Weeknd. A dedication to a more mature image saw the emergence of guitar-rock on 'Dangerous Woman' before hitting stuttering club beats on 'Into You'. This sense that genre is something that Grande and her collaborators are happy to play and experiment with in each album cycle has lent a certain unpredictability to her music. Listening to the experimental alt-pop of 'Sweetener', you could never guess that in less than a year, she'd be spitting bars over trap beats and emulating mumble-rap on songs like '7 Rings'.

But take into account that one of Grande's biggest influences on her artistry is the English experimental alt-pop icon Imogen Heap, a singer-songwriter and producer formerly of the electronic duo Frou Frou, known for her madcap and experimentalist approach to pop music.

As a vocalist, Ariana also clearly wanted to emulate the likes of Mariah Carey and Whitney Houston on her earlier material and her commitment to never staying in one musical lane clearly calls back to the work of Madonna, a future collaborator of Grande's, as well as the often-overlooked experimentalism of much of Britney Spears' boldest albums, like *In The Zone* and *Blackout*.

At the time of writing, Ariana Grande has nine US Number 1 singles, six US Number 1 albums, two Grammys, one Oscar nomination and life-time Spotify streams now totalling over 53 billion (a number that will continue to rise).

By and large, the dominant theme of pop music in the third decade of the twenty-first century is a fixation on, and a search for, authenticity. Artists like Billie Eilish, SZA and more recently, Charli xcx, have all been lauded for the honesty contained in their music and how it connects to not just their core fanbases, but the public at large. I would argue that, certainly as pure pop acts go, few are as bracingly authentic as Grande. Her best work directly references traumatic, sometimes even horrifying events in her personal life, like the Manchester bombing of 2017, which turned her into something of a folk hero in the UK, the death of her former partner, rapper Mac Miller, and the impact it had on not just her relationship with then-fiancé Pete Davidson but her music career at large, and the recent divorce from her husband of three years, Dalton Gomez. She tackles all these topics with unrestrained candour, something that has opened her artistry into hitherto undiscovered highs.

In this journey through her life, music and acting, we will discover the work of an artist, an actress, a *vocalist*, a songwriter and now a producer in her own right who has made some of the best pop music of the last twenty years by staying true to *exactly* who she is.

This is Ariana Grande . . . and we must thank her for it.

# I

# Career Beginnings and *Victorious*

Every big pop girl has to start somewhere . . .

While it's always nice to think of the journey to pop stardom as akin to Dorothy being plucked from Kansas and dropped into the technicolour world of Oz by way of a tornado, the ascent to the upper echelons of the kind of celebrity Ariana Grande has endured for now more than half of her life is not the result of serendipity. Instead, it's the payout of years of hard work and blind luck, oftentimes behind the scenes and more times than not without the promise of instant success.

You see the Ariana Grande you know and love? With the high ponytail and the bangers? Though it might seem like it, she didn't arrive overnight. She – like most of her peers – was working from a very young age and had a star persona that was carefully curated behind the scenes, years before she even began releasing music.

It's a hard path to navigate, full of pitfalls at every turn. For every Ariana Grande or, say, Miley Cyrus or Selena Gomez, there are countless examples of former children's television stars who tried – and failed – to make the transition into a full-time music career; Grande's *Victorious* co-star Victoria Justice, for one, whose own foray into a solo career, despite being the main character of *Victorious*, failed to make an impact.

While many casual fans would point to Ariana's starring role as Cat Valentine on the Nickelodeon sitcom *Victorious* as the genesis of her career, she got her start before most of her peers had even begun studying their times tables. Like a little Rachel Berry, Ariana Grande made her cultural debut as an actress on Broadway, working on the musical *13* aged just fifteen years old.

What is *13*, I hear you ask? It's a musical with music and lyrics by Jason Robert Brown (who would collaborate with Grande once more on a bonus track on *Dangerous Woman*) and a book by Dan Elish and Robert Horn, concerning teenager Evan Goldman, who moves from New York to Ohio as his parents are divorcing and trying to prepare for his upcoming Bar Mitzvah. *13*'s big draw was the fact that its entire cast was made up of teenagers. Grande made her Broadway debut in the role of Charlotte and starred alongside her future *Victorious* co-star Elizabeth (Liz) Gillies, with the two fast becoming lifelong friends. In September 2008, *13* opened on Broadway and closed after 105 performances and twenty previews in January 2009. But don't feel too sad for Ariana, her big break was finally on the way.

The year 2009 was also when she was cast in *Victorious*. The conceit of *Victorious* is this: Tori Vega

(Victoria Justice), an aspiring singer who wins a place at a performing arts high school, also attended by her older sister Trina (Daniella Monet) and a host of side-characters, including mean girl frenemy Jade (Gillies), heartthrob and quasi-love interest Beck (Avan Jogia) and Cat Valentine, the role that would be taken by Grande.

She was the most consistent and well-rounded performer of the troupe. Cat Valentine falls into the Phoebe from *Friends* or the April from *Parks and Recreation* mould; a side-character that, while not really fulfilling any of the main plots of the series, is always within the orbit of the main players and is the source of much comical relief. In Cat's case, this was through her being well meaning and endearing but also stupid. Despite her young age, Ariana played her with gusto; her performance is broad, but at times intensely studied, involving more acting than you think a children's television sitcom might contain.

But Ariana's casting in *Victorious* had wide-ranging implications. When the show first began to air in 2010, we were living in a post-*High School Musical* landscape. The recent boom of the musical dramedy *Glee* also inspired the show; much like *Glee*, the songs featured on *Victorious* and sung by its cast could be purchased as digital singles. This almost instantaneous access, exposed even further by the then fast-expanding use of social media sites like Twitter (X) turned Grande and her cast mates into teen idols. Much like any wannabe starlet in the spotlight for the first time, she made the most of this moment.

This was Ariana's first taste of celebrity but she was already deploying savvy business tactics to expand her identity outside of *Victorious*. Her frank, open discussions with fans on Twitter and frequent covers on YouTube quickly started earning her a fanbase, the 'Arianators'.

To hear Grande tell the story herself, despite her burgeoning fame as a teen idol, music was *always* her priority. Even as a teenager she realised she had to play a long game to get exactly what she wanted.

'I never really saw myself as an actress,' she once told *Vogue*, 'but when I started talking about wanting to make R&B music at fourteen, they were like, "What the fuck would you sing about? This is never going to work. You should audition for some TV shows and build yourself a platform and get yourself out there, because you're funny and cute and you should do that until you're old enough to make the music you want to make." So I did that. I booked that TV show, and then I was like, OK, *now* can I make music?'

While most of her *Victorious* castmates, like Victoria Justice, ended up contractually signing to Sony, who distributed the show's original music, Ariana seemed to always have one eye ahead into the future and had a 'carve out' clause in her contract, essentially meaning she could sign to a label of her choice.

She found that label in the form of Republic Records which, in 2025, is home to superstars like Taylor Swift,

The Weeknd and Nicki Minaj – the latter two would be future collaborators. Grande was signed to the label after its CEO, Monte Lipman, was sent some of her YouTube covers by a friend. Impressed by those covers, designed to show off her impressive vocal range and her magnetic star power, he signed her to a recording contract in August 2011, aged eighteen.

As Lipman tells it, even as a teenager with little professional experience in the music industry, Ariana was determined to make herself heard.

'I'm pitching her [on Republic],' he recalls. 'About twelve minutes in, she shuts me down. "Do you want to hear me sing?" Then she belts [out] a Whitney track and just stops time.'

It seems that even in 2011, Grande was beginning to play the long game with her career. 'Ari is very determined and incredibly resourceful,' Lipman continued. 'She said she [only] pursued acting [on *Victorious*] to set up her music career.'[1]

What did that music sound like? Well . . .

GEORGE GRIFFITHS

## 'PUT YOUR HEARTS UP'

**Release date:** 12 December 2011
**Written by:** Linda Perry, Martin Johnson, Matt Squire
**Produced by:** Matt Squire

The saying goes that 'everyone has to start somewhere' but maybe Ariana Grande would prefer you to forget that she started here.

Her disdain for her debut solo single – a bubblegum pop confection that contains a heavy interpolation of 4 Non-Blondes' 1993 classic, 'What's Up' – is well recorded. In fact, when her second studio album *My Everything* and its accompanying singles blew up into a chart force, Grande forced her label to hide the track's music video from her YouTube channel although it is still unlisted and available to watch, should the mood ever take you.

So, why does she hate 'Put Your Hearts Up' so much? Horrible title aside, as far as starting guns on careers go, it's certainly no 'Crazy In Love' or '. . . Baby One More Time'. In fact, the one thing you can say about 'Put Your Hearts Up' is that it knows its audience – children.

Yes, it's a perfectly serviceable synth-pop track, with a very of-the-moment production that veers ever so slightly close to EDM. Grande's register is lower than you might expect and a smattering of stuttering vocals gives a small glimpse into, perhaps, an attempt at making it more mature than something you would hear on *Glee* or

*Kidz Bop.* Nevertheless, as an introduction to Ariana as an artist, 'Put Your Hearts Up' tells us little about who she is; ironic, considering her later material would be so personable.

In fact, it seems on reflection that 'Put Your Hearts Up' is not a release by Ariana Grande herself, but rather Ariana Grande pretending to play Cat Valentine, her character on *Victorious*. But God loves a trier, so let's dive in! What is 'Put Your Hearts Up' trying to say? Well, it seems built around the emerging trend at that time of using your fingers to make a heart, which was fast becoming *de rigueur* at both pop concerts and across burgeoning social media sites like Twitter and Tumblr. The song's saccharine belief in self-love – and sharing that love with everyone around you, whether they want it or not – does slot in nicely to a short-lived trend in pop music at that time. Bolstered by the themes of acceptance and diversity in television shows like *Glee*, which quickly became a phenomenon in the US around its debut in 2009, we soon saw several pop songs try to dial into this cultural moment.

Chief of these would be Lady Gaga's gay rights anthem 'Born This Way', of course, and a twin collection of singles by P!nk, 'Raise Your Glass' and 'Fuckin' Perfect', as well as Sara Bareilles' 'Brave' and Katy Perry's 'Roar'. 'Put Your Hearts Up' definitely fits into this category, although it wasn't as distinctive as 'Born This Way' in its message.

Lyrically, too, we're not talking Lennon-McCartney

levels of composition here either. During the track's second verse, there's the barmy reference to not being able to resurrect Gandhi or Martin Luther King Jr. But did you know that's OK? Because we can do anything! Tell 'em, Queen! Luckily, that particular statement is stuck under so much reverb, you can hardly make sense of what Ariana's saying.

Now, let's talk about the track's music video. There's a reason that Grande wanted her label to hide it from her YouTube profile – it's not very good. By her own admission, speaking around the release of 'Problem', she said that her issues stemmed from the fact the song was 'geared towards kids [. . .] and felt inauthentic and fake,' she told *Rolling Stone* in a 2014 cover profile. 'It was the worst moment of my life. For the video, they gave me a bad spray tan and put me in a princess dress and made me frolic down the street. That whole thing was straight out of hell.'[2]

Ariana's opinion on the track does seem to have cooled in the ensuing years, however. In 2020, she explained her disdain for the song at that time came from a place of self-doubt; she was worried that her core audience still saw her as Cat from *Victorious* and would expect her to make bubblegum pop.

Maybe that would have been the case for her core group of fans, but 'Put Your Hearts Up' wasn't mature enough to truly break through. Upon release, it failed to chart on the Billboard Hot 100 or any of its affiliate charts, although by 2014, Billboard noted that the single had shifted 500,000 copies in total in the US, combined through both digital downloads and streams.

There's an outdated notion that, in pop music especially, you only get one chance at a good first impression. I'd like to debunk that theory. 'Put Your Hearts Up' is proof that *anyone* can have a second chance . . . as long the music is good.

## 'POPULAR SONG' with Mika

**Release date:** 21 December 2012
**Written by:** Mika, Priscilla Renea, Mathieu Jomphe, Stephen Schwartz
**Produced by:** Greg Wells, Mika, Jason Nevins

A year ago, the concept of anyone caring about a one-off single Ariana Grande once appeared on with the UK singer-songwriter Mika (yes, of 'Grace Kelly' fame) that was released to precisely no success whatsoever would be inconceivable. But now? 'Popular Song' doesn't look like a minor bump on Grande's road to stardom anymore, it kind of looks like destiny manifest.

I'd never thought I'd say this, but let's talk about 'Popular Song'!

The song's origins have nothing to do with Grande herself. One can only imagine her involvement was spawned out of a notion to re-introduce Mika's music to a younger audience, while also continuing to prop up a prospective solo launch for Ariana. 'Popular Song' was her only release in more than a year, following the muted reception to 'Put Your Hearts Up'.

Originally, 'Popular Song' was included on Mika's third studio album, *The Origin of Love* (2012), as an album track featuring the songwriter Priscilla Renea. Renea now records under the moniker Muni Long, but at the time was a hitmaker for the likes of The Saturdays, Fifth Harmony and Cheryl Cole. Melodically, it's basically a completely different track and contains more explicit language, although it does retain the sample of 'Popular' from the film *Wicked*.

For its single release, it was clear something more was needed. Mika wanted it to emulate the 'wonky pop' of his breakthrough hit single, 'Grace Kelly' and so the track was reworked and restructured with producer Jason Nevins to make it more standard Top 40 fare. Including some rewrites, and now-added vocals from Grande, a new version of 'Popular Song' was born.

The conceit of 'Popular Song' is the classic 'revenge' number. It's concerned with Mika and Ariana reflecting on their humble beginnings and all the people who used to look down on them, but now find themselves *looking up* at a pair of stars on the rise. Perhaps the most comical couplet of the song comes from Mika music that someone used to cheerlead, but now they work at the cinema making 'popular corn', which is certainly one way of putting it!

The inclusion of 'Popular' here is rather inspired. *Wicked* is something we will (obviously) get into a little later down the line in Grande's career, but in the context of the original musical (and its later live-action film), the song is sung by Glinda, who promises to turn Elphaba, the future Wicked Witch of the West, into a 'popular' girl like herself during their time at Shiz University.

Knowing this context, it's quite clear that 'Popular Song' is rather an inversion of 'Popular' – instead of helping make someone else popular, Mika and Ariana are now looking down at the people who *thought* they were popular, but life has turned out quite differently.

I don't know if you've ever watched the music video for 'Popular Song', but if you haven't seen it in a while, I would recommend you watch it again, just because at points, I can't believe what I'm seeing. Directed by Chris Marrs Piliero, who would also go on to direct the visuals for 'Break Free', it has a definite influence of the Addams Family and the work of Tim Burton, casting Mika and Ariana as two beleaguered high school students. This works for Grande – she was nineteen at the time. As for Mika . . . Well, it's giving 'how are you doing, fellow kids?' Their dastardly plan is to enact revenge on their bullies by brewing a potion that turns them to stone. There's a little twist ending, too, when Grande's character seems to remember Mika being mean to her when they were children. Are their characters relatives? Friends? Lovers? I have absolutely no idea. All I know is, Grande turns *him* to stone too.

At the time, 'Popular Song' probably made sense for Grande's career as a burgeoning pop star. She was a year out from her debut single stalling, *Victorious* was airing its fourth and final season and she was clearly juggling those prior commitments with retooling her own music. A new collaboration would keep several of those fires burning and keep her in the mainstream conversation. Although, let's be clear, she was collaborating with *Mika*, not Ed Sheeran.

Looking back at it now, though, just breeds more

questions than answers. Did Mika and Ariana Grande know who each other were before they recorded this duet together? I very much doubt it. Have they ever hung out since promoting it together? I would bet money against it!

The most interesting thing about 'Popular Song' now, of course, is its direct link to *Wicked*. Looking back, do you think people listening to 'Popular Song' in 2012 were aware the pint-sized pop princess featured on the track would, more than a decade later, be up for an actual *Oscar* for playing Glinda?

If you say yes, I know you're lying!

Much like 'Put Your Hearts Up', 'Popular Song' didn't really have much of an impact charts-wise, although it did become Grande's first entry on the Billboard Hot 100 as a solo artist, peaking at Number 87. Surprisingly, despite Mika's higher profile in his native UK, the song entirely failed to chart there.

The duo's promotional efforts included a perky live performance on *Dancing With The Stars*, where it *does* seem like they only met backstage for a few seconds before being thrown onstage together and forced to perform. It's cute! Plus, it's the start of Ariana beginning to wear cat ears – a signature look that would become a staple throughout the *My Everything* era. However, better things were on the horizon. The next year would not just bring about the ending of *Victorious*, but the start of Grande's career as a pop star proper.

# 2

# *Yours Truly* and the Beginnings of a Pop Career

There are no guarantees in the life of a pop star. In fact, you could argue that most of the great pop careers thrived in the face of oncoming failure.

It took Madonna two records until she scored her first Number 1 single, 'Like A Virgin' (1984), Lady Gaga and Katy Perry were both dropped from their first record deals and more recently, Dua Lipa veered very close to the dumper. Her first undeniable hit, 'New Rules' (2017), was released at the end of a seven-single run.

Ariana Grande was no different. In fact, as work began on her debut album, the chips were already stacked against her. 'Put Your Hearts Up', the first attempt to launch her pop career, was DOA and it looked – even if only for a second – that things might not go her way. But, like all the best divas, she had a point to prove and nothing was going to stop her.

First, though, it was time to take stock of what had gone wrong so far. As we know, 'Put Your Hearts Up' did *not* seem like the musical debut of Ariana Grande, but instead her fictional alter-ego, Cat Valentine. Acknowledging this would be important, as would be finding the best foot forward. Even at the tender age of twenty, Grande showed a shrewd understanding of where things stood and pop music as a business transaction. She knew an evolution was needed; the music she released would need to resonate and to do that, it would have to come from the heart. People can always smell a fake. Now was the time to show them what she could *really* do.

To their credit, Ariana's label Republic Records seemed to be aware of her considerable potential and the fact that she *wasn't* dropped following the relative failure of both 'Put Your Hearts Up' (that 4 Non-Blondes' sample couldn't have been cheap!) and 'Popular' is telling. The pop graveyard is littered with the careers of would-be starlets who were unceremoniously dropped from their deals after their first singles failed to resonate, Grande's *Victorious* co-star Victoria Justice being one of them.

Instead, in 2013 Grande came to Republic with a plan. Her vision for her debut album wasn't one of throwaway electronic pop tracks, but a vintage R&B record, influenced by the likes of Motown Records, Whitney Houston and most importantly, Mariah Carey's sterling 1990s album run, from *Emotions* to *Butterfly*. Carey is a pivotal figure in Grande's career, Ariana herself having called her 'the queen of my life'.[1]

This was inspired thinking, but also carried a heavy

risk (like most correct decisions do). In 2013, pop at large was *not* interested in looking to the past, it was still deep in conversation with the EDM boom of the late '00s-early '10s, and its greatest female stars dealt heavily in maximalism, not vintage pastiche.

The year 2013 was the year that Lady Gaga and Katy Perry released *ARTPOP* and *Prism* respectively. *Prism* would score Perry two Number 1 hits, while *ARTPOP*'s chaos would send Gaga on a spiral that it would take her at least half a decade to recover from. One thing became clear in 2013: pop's new guard was slowly beginning to take control. In that year, Miley Cyrus dominated headlines with her most controversial record, *Bangerz*, and Lorde seemingly came out of nowhere with the generational anthem, *Royals*. Grande may not have known this at the time, but it was the perfect time for her to re-emerge with a new image and sound.

With considerable hindsight, *now* we can view *Yours Truly*, Ariana's debut album, as an extremely successful move, but at the time, she was going against the cultural grain. Yet, the biggest risks almost always come with the biggest reward . . . *if* you get it right.

Getting it right was not just important, but imperative. If she was going to pull this vision off, Ariana would need to find the right collaborators. So often, what failed pop records have in common is not whether their concept is good or not, but whether this concept is brought to life in the best way possible. This is something that rings true for most of her later career, too. Grande has a knack for working with the right producers and writers at the right time and for the right project.

For *Yours Truly*, Ariana made a conscious effort not to work with the hitmakers of that time (she'd save that for her *next* album!) but instead a crack team of collaborators who truly understood the references she wished to pull from. Chiefly, these were Harmony Samuels, an English producer who had previously worked with the likes of Janet Jackson, Ciara and Jennifer Lopez, Kenneth 'Babyface' Edmonds, one of the most famous producers from R&B's 1990s heyday, who had worked with everyone from Mariah to Madonna and Tommy Brown, a then-unknown up-and-comer who was to become one of the most important creative partners in Ariana's artistic growth, along with the songwriter Victoria Monét, who also earns her first credits for a Grande project on *Yours Truly*.

'Ariana is a special one,' Samuels remembered of their time together. 'She's very in control of her stuff. She told me what she wanted to do.'[2]

The social capital Grande had built up during her time in *Victorious* also finally started to pay off in dividends. Upon its release, *Yours Truly* topped the Billboard 200, gifting Ariana her first Number 1 album. Critical reception was also incredibly warm; the album even received a cautiously optimistic 6.5 rating from indie gatekeepers Pitchfork,[3] signalling that Grande was on the right side of both pop fans and critics alike.

This number one album would become the first of

many. The fact that it was such a success straight out the gate marked Grande immediately as one-to-watch, and as a record, *Yours Truly* really does set its stall out well. The run of its first eight tracks is somewhat extraordinary: a clear attempt to recreate the pop and verve of the best '90s R&B records, but with an eye to modernisation too. The melodies are tight, the hooks are iron-clad, and, for the first time, Grande finally seemed to figure out who she was as an artist: a *vocalist*, first and foremost, who was just as comfortable referencing the past as she was existing in pop's present.

Nothing would be a better representation of this than *Yours Truly*'s first single, the first quantifiable hit of Grande's career, and it would see the start of a personal connection which would have repercussions throughout the rest of her life.

ARIANA GRANDE

## 'THE WAY' with Mac Miller

**Release date:** 26 March 2013
**Written by:** Harmony Samuels, Amber Streeter, A-Rod, Jordin Sparks, Mac Miller, Brenda Russell
**Produced by:** Harmony Samuels

Ariana would like you to think of 'The Way' as her debut single proper. Taking what we know about 'Put Your Hearts Up' aside, it really *does* feel like the first full single by Ariana Grande herself to enter the world.

Twelve years after its initial release, it's still amazing how much 'Grande'-ness seems to have been captured in 'The Way'. Out of all her early works, it seemed like *this* was the sound that she has been fighting her way back to, slowly but surely, throughout her career. However, I say this knowing that, despite sounding like the true arrival of Ariana Grande, the lead single from her debut album was not actually written with Ariana in mind. Instead, 'The Way' first came to life through Samuels' work with Jordin Sparks, a former *American Idol* winner who had scored a few hits in the mid-00s, most notably 'No Air' with Chris Brown (bop).

Sparks' well-documented issues with her label at the time are probably why 'The Way' was never released by her. The first time Ariana Grande heard 'The Way' was when Samuels played it for her during a session. Captivated by the beat, which samples Big Pun's 1998 song, 'Still Not A Player', itself a containing a sample of

Brenda Russell's 1979 track, 'A Little Bit Of Love' (Russell retains a songwriting credit for that original sample), it's easy to see why Ariana was so excited.

'When she [first came to my studio], she played me [her demos],' Samuels said of his first meeting with Grande when 'The Way' was born. 'They weren't bad, I was just like "Your voice is bigger than your records. Your voice isn't being highlighted by the records. You need a big song."'[4]

Samuels wasn't wrong. 'The Way' was exactly what Ariana had been looking for: a track that could easily have fitted on an early-career record by Whitney Houston. In my humble opinion, it would have slipped easily into Mariah Carey's *Emotions* – please take that as a huge compliment. But to call 'The Way' *just* a throwback record would be insincere. It was conversation with R&B's past just as much as it was with hip-hop's present – why else do you think it has a Mac Miller feature?!

Mac Miller (real name Malcolm McCormick) was, at the time of 'The Way's debut, one of the fastest-rising rappers on this scene. He had already released two mixtapes and his 2011 debut album, *Blue Slide Park*, had hit Number 1 on the Billboard 200 albums chart, becoming the first independently distributed album to do so in US chart history. But one thing Mac Miller was lacking in 2013? A quantifiable hit single. 'The Way' was a handy antidote to that. In fact, as Ariana Grande tells it, when she first played Miller her demo of 'The Way' and asked him to cut a verse, his response was, 'Sounds like a hit to me.'[5]

It's clear that Grande believed in 'The Way' from the off. So much so that she shot its lo-fi music video featuring herself and Miller in a balloon-filled room without the assistance of her label. Instead, she filmed it with a friend, Jones Crow, as the director and her troupe of dancers. Grande and Mac Miller end the video by kissing, a gentle reminder to the audience that Ariana wasn't a child star anymore.

The energy of 'The Way' was electric. Republic Records' VP Charlie Walk, as he tells it, first heard the song when it was blasting out of CEO Monte Lipman's office, where he'd been watching the DIY video Grande had just made. Walk then 'immediately' made the decision to release 'The Way' as a single and the lead cut from *Yours Truly*.[6]

It turns out Mac Miller was right: 'The Way' was indeed a hit. In fact, the track debuted at Number 9 on the Billboard Hot 100, shifting 219,000 digital downloads in its first week on sale (including an eye-popping 120,000 in just two days). It became both Grande's and Miller's first Top 10 single in the US. But how did Ariana go from the relative failure of 'Put Your Hearts Up', which didn't chart anywhere, to a Top 10 debut? To put it in simple terms, she learnt how to market herself effectively in this new age of social media and fandom. Her guerilla marketing campaign tactics of teasing the song and its music video on her Twitter account clearly engaged the Arianators enough to click 'buy' on iTunes. Unlike 'Put Your Hearts Up', 'The Way' wasn't engineered to simply engage the child viewers of *Victorious*.

Much like Grande, in the four years since the series debuted, they'd grown up and like most teenagers will tell you, they don't like being talked down to or perceived as immature. 'The Way' was the first sign that Ariana realised her audience was growing up with her and they responded to this call to arms.

The Way's chart debut was also historic; Ariana Grande became the first female act to make her chart debut inside the Top 10 in five years. The song also set a record that she still holds, as the female act with every lead single from her albums debuting in the US Top 10. I don't know what that proves, but it sounds impressive, right?

Now, in the space of just a few weeks, Grande had gone from being an untested pop ingénue to a genuine chart success. She was, officially, in the game and the aftershock of this impressive beginning would put her firmly on the popstar hamster wheel; a never-ending cycle of recording, release, promotion and touring that she wouldn't be able to escape for the next five years.

Even outside of that, the effects 'The Way' had on her career were astounding. Not just musically, either. Years after they collaborated on the song, Grande and Miller would strike up a relationship in 2016. For Grande herself, it seemed that the pipeline from friends to lovers was inevitable. Upon Miller's death from a drug overdose in

2018, she said in an Instagram post, 'I adored you from the day I met you when I was 19.'[7]

'The Way' stands as a testament to believing in yourself and your vision. In the hall of great pop debuts, it may not hold a candle to the likes of '. . . Baby One More Time' or even 'Royals', but what it *did* do was set Grande up extraordinarily well. If her career path proves *anything*, it's that good things come to those who wait.

## 'BABY I'

**Release date:** 22 July 2013
**Written by:** Babyface, Antonio Dixon, J. Que
**Produced by:** Babyface

If you're going to make a pastiche record of '90s hip-hop and R&B, it should be a rule that you need to involve Babyface. As both a producer, songwriter and an artist in his own right, Kenneth 'Babyface' Edmonds has put claim to some of the genre's defining works. He helped shape Whitney Houston's best album, *I'm Your Baby Tonight* (1990), worked on TLC's generation-defining *CrazySexyCool* (1994) and his sole collaboration with Madonna, 'Take A Bow' (1994), still holds the record for the Queen of Pop's longest-ever running Number 1 hit in the US (seven weeks – fact, fans).

Babyface records carry their own panache and signature style. He is a student and a lover of the old Motown Records, influenced by the music of Diana Ross & The Supremes so it would be obvious that on a record paying tribute to exactly the kind of music Babyface made in his heyday as a hitmaker, he would be involved here. Much like 'The Way', however, *Yours Truly*'s second single, 'Baby I', was not created initially with Ariana Grande in mind. Instead, Babyface imagined someone entirely different as the vocalist on his track – Queen Beyoncé herself!

As these things go, 'Baby I' did *not* go to Beyoncé. We don't know if she ever recorded, or even heard, the song. Instead, it found its way to Ariana who, unlike Bey, was *not* in a position to turn down a cut from one of the most iconic producers of his time.

As a follow-up to 'The Way', 'Baby I' makes a lot of sense and builds upon the foundations set by its predecessor. It's a lot less 'modern' than 'The Way', instead it *really* leans into those vintage vibes Grande was so keen to channel into her work at the time.

Lyrically, we're on much of the same page as 'The Way' – with Ariana paying tribute to her lover with a specific kind of doe-eyed devotion only a nineteen-year-old can accurately muster. In an interview with *Complex* in 2013, Grande revealed that it was actually Mac Miller who persuaded her to release 'Baby I' as the next single from *Yours Truly*.

'I was sceptical [of its potential as a single],' she told *Complex*. 'But I loved the song just because it feels a lot like *Dreamgirls* to me.'[8]

Unfortunately for Miller, he didn't quite have the same foresight here as he did with 'The Way'. Still, Babyface makes a lot of room for Grande and her voice on 'Baby I'. She sounds great, her vocals are big, full and absolutely packed with emotion. It's also nice to hear what she would have sounded like on a classic Babyface record if she'd been around in the '90s. The production is probably my favourite part of 'Baby I'; it is meticulously crafted and very evocative of a golden age for the genre. It's also quietly strange – at points, it veers into full-on New Jack Swing.

Ariana sounds fantastic, but what is clear is that she is at a distance on the track. We know it wasn't written for her, for one, and her vocals are even more egregiously Mariah-esque here than they are on 'The Way', with the backing vocals sounding straight from a Toni Braxton record. Where 'The Way' sounds like a tribute to the divas Grande wanted to emulate, 'Baby I' veers too closely into imitation.

For an artist who would come to be defined by how personal and authentic her music is, 'Baby I' feels oddly anonymous today. Then again, maybe that's just a testament to how far Ariana Grande has come along in her artistry. Also, did you know that this wasn't the last time she would record a Beyoncé cast-off? 'R.E.M.' from *Sweetener* was originally written by Pharrell for inclusion on *Beyoncé*, before getting retooled.

ARIANA GRANDE

## 'RIGHT THERE' with Big Sean

**Release date:** 6 August 2013
**Written by:** Ariana Grande, Harmony Samuels, Carmen Reece, J 'Lonny' Bereal, James 'J-Doe' Smith, A-Rod, Big Sean, Jeff Lorber
**Produced by:** Harmony Samuels

'[People] think I'm a badass now.'[9] This was Ariana Grande's reaction to the news that she was linking up with another rapper for her next single, a semi-sequel to breakout hit 'The Way' and the biggest hint yet that she was ready for the big leagues.

There comes a very specific point – normally towards the end of one promo cycle and the burgeoning start of a new era – where things can seem to shift. It happened in 2024 with Sabrina Carpenter, for instance. Her superstar-making hit, 'Espresso', wouldn't have been possible without the release of the slyly suggestive 'Nonsense' and 'Feather' the year prior. People may *seem* to explode out of nowhere, but in actual fact most of pop's biggest breakout acts have been quietly working in the background for years.

We're coming very quickly to the point in Ariana Grande's career where she took off like a rocket. The signs were always there – even if you squint hard enough, you can see them in 'Put Your Hearts Up' – but as the cycle for *Yours Truly* wrapped up, the concept of Ariana Grande: Pop star was no longer just this ephemeral thought waiting to come to life – it was manifest!

'Right There' was the last single to be released from *Yours Truly* and the last release from Grande before she became a pop force to be reckoned with. In one way, this is the end of one story – of Ariana Grande, the ingénue with a song in her heart and a point to prove – and the beginning of another: of *Ariana Grande*, one of the most successful recording artists of her era. So, let's pay witness to this together, shall we?

Grande has said herself that she views 'Right There' to be a sequel, or at least a continuation, of sorts to 'The Way'. You can definitely see why she would make this connection: both tracks are interested in combining the throwback production of *Yours Truly* with the injection of a verse from one of rap's brightest stars at the time.

In 2013, Big Sean (real name Sean Michael Leonard Anderson) was on a hot streak. Signed to Kanye West's GOOD Music imprint as a teenager, Sean had by that point broken big with his first two studio album, 2011's *Finally Famous* and 2013's *Hall of Fame* earning Top 3 debuts on the Billboard 200 album charts. He was already making waves as a hitmaker too; he'd collaborated with Nicki Minaj on 'Dance (A$$)', his first Top 10 as a lead artist, and had made a bigger impression on the younger generation with his guest verse on Justin Bieber's 2012 single, 'As Long As You Love Me'. Bieber and Grande have a lot of shared history, having both been managed by Scooter Braun for the majority of their careers; Grande had supported Bieber on 2013's Believe Tour and the two would later go on to collaborate on the 2020 Number 1 single, 'Stuck With U'.

A lot of people sat up and took notice of Big Sean in 2013, Ariana Grande being one of them. The fact the pair entered into an eight-month-long relationship a year later is no surprise, listening to their palpable chemistry on 'Right There'. Although their time together was relatively short, Grande told the *Telegraph* in 2014 that she 'thought the world' of Sean, even going so far as to call him 'one of the most amazing men in the world . . . and that includes my brother and grandfather'.[10]

Like most 'ex-acts', the transition Ariana experienced from a child to adult star was fraught with landmines. It's no coincidence that *Yours Truly*'s aesthetics are about as far away as you can imagine from Miley Cyrus's *Bangerz*, another former teen idol who was determined to drag her audience with her, kicking and screaming, into her adult years. *Bangerz* was brash and chaotic and totally on Cyrus's own terms. It was a brilliant strategy, but it wasn't a one-fits-all policy for her peers. Grande was much less obvious and insistent at this time of signposting her growing maturity. She wasn't exactly shaving her hair off and parading on the VMAs stage with a foam finger. Instead, her growth would be subtler. Slower. She tiptoes around the concept of her becoming a more grown-up artist throughout *Yours Truly* and it's something she wouldn't fully engage with until a few years later with *Dangerous Woman*. You can hear this hesitation to engage with more mature themes in the material.

'Right There' perhaps repeated the formula of 'The Way' a bit *too* well to strike out on its own. The track debuted and peaked at a disappointing Number 84 on the Billboard Hot 100 and missed the Top 100 on the UK Official Singles Chart entirely. However, 'The Way' had successfully broken Grande through the mainstream music market and *Yours Truly* was already her first Number 1 album. Similar success for 'Right There' would have been nice, of course, but Ariana was already on to bigger and better things. She had a tour to prepare for one and was already recording the more pop-focused material for her second album with storied hitmaker Max Martin.

Reaching the next echelon of pop stardom wouldn't be a problem.

# 3

# *My Everything* and the Journey to 'It Girl' Status

If you want to make it – *truly* make it – on the main stage, then there comes a point in every pop star's career where one must surrender to the machine. I wish it wasn't like this. That stardom didn't require some form of prerequisite sacrifice (there are outliers to this theory, like Kate Bush and Lorde, but by and large, they are just that, outliers), but it's a reality we must face.

*My Everything*, the record that turned Ariana Grande into pop's undisputed new 'It Girl', is a complete 180-degree turn from *Yours Truly*. The kind of from-the-ground-up reinvention only a 21-year-old can pull off with total confidence. An album of mostly electronic pop bangers, it riffs as much on EDM and synth-pop as *Yours Truly* did on R&B and doo-wop.

It's also a much more collaborative record; almost every track contains a feature from of-the-moment buzz artists like Iggy Azalea, Childish Gambino and The Weeknd. The roster of producers and writers attached is also more expansive; the only collaborators to return from the previous era would be Tommy Brown and Victoria Monét, with Ariana swapping Harmony Samuels and Babyface for the true commercial hitmakers of the era: Max Martin and his Wolf Cousins cohort; a company of mostly Swedish writers and producers, a number of whom, such as Ilya Salmanzadeh and Savan Kotecha, along with Martin himself, have returned again and again to Grande's musical world.

*My Everything* is a shining example of when everything – from recording to single releases to the music videos to live performances – clicks in perfect harmony. Most artists are lucky to get this to happen just once in their career, but for Grande this was to happen twice.

The new album came around quickly. It was released on 22 August 2014, just under twelve months after *Yours Truly*, which dropped on 30 August 2013. The speed of this is uncanny, but there's one simple reason for it: you have to strike while the iron's hot. Indeed, even just a month out from her debut album's release, Ariana told *Rolling Stone* she was already recording new material, something that she wanted to be an 'evolution'.[1]

It turned out to be not just an evolution of sound, but of style too. After all, Ariana was now twenty-one years old. Gone were the cute vintage styles and babydoll dresses, in came the now-Grande signatures – a high ponytail so high it had its own fixed centre of gravity, tight mini-skirts and platform stiletto boots that made her look less like a lounge singer and more like a warrior from the planet Glamazon. These were to become essential touchstones in her pop star iconography going forward. Sure, they would be elevated, substituted or sometimes even removed altogether in the ensuing years, but these are the core ingredients of her public persona. The stock of who 'Ariana Grande' is to most of the public.

In case I haven't made it quite clear, *My Everything* was an event record. The event being Grande herself. Despite the presence of the planet's biggest hitmakers, it's amazing how present she feels at the centre of this record. This is one of the shocking things about *My Everything*. It is both a stunning collection of hit singles resting alongside some filler tracks but also a solid, varied and at times extremely impressive pop album at the same time.

There's an ease and fluidity to Grande's vision of pop music here. It's able to switch from high-tempo bangers ('Problem'), slinky EDM ('Break Free'), seductive synth-pop ('Love Me Harder') and elegiac electronica ('One Last Time', still one of the best songs she has ever put her name to). And those are just the hits! Further down on *My Everything*, we have the title track, a lovelorn ballad that reunites her with Tommy Brown and Victoria Monét, the hip-hop leaning 'Hands On Me' with A$AP Mob member A$AP Ferg and then the Harry Styles-penned 'Just A Little Bit Of Your Heart'.

It can easily be said that every album Ariana Grande makes after *My Everything* functions as a loose concept record. *Dangerous Woman* is about her own growth as a woman and an artist, *Sweetener* is concerned with how to heal in real time, *Thank U, Next* is her most concept-heavy – a record of emancipation, grief and celebration, and wondering if it's OK that all these states can exist together at the same time. *Positions* is her marriage record and, well, *Eternal Sunshine* is her divorce one. The concept of *My Everything* is that there is no concept. The title isn't a lie, it's a promise; she is throwing everything *and* the kitchen sink at the wall and seeing what sticks. It's alarming how much of it does.

This *was* a surrender to the pop machine, make no doubt about it, but it was also a sacrifice with a clear reward. After *My Everything*, Ariana would never *not* be a celebrity again (for better or worse).

You can see this in action; this was the first era where her personal life began to be used for tabloid fodder. Her first big public relationship, with Australian YouTuber Jai Brooks of the Janoskians, broke down just before the album's release in August 2014 after two years. Grande hit headlines for moving on quite quickly with British musician Nathan Sykes of pop band The Wanted (the pair collaborated on the 2013 single 'Almost Is Never Enough' and also at the time shared management) before getting together with Big Sean in October 2014.

One thing a record label can't buy you is publicity. By 2014, Ariana was getting a *lot* of it. You could almost feel the music industry making way to accommodate her. From *My Everything* alone, she scored four consecutive

US Top 10 singles, including 'Bang Bang', which was included as a bonus track on the LP despite technically belonging to Jessie J – but we'll get to that! The record also became her second to hit Number 1 in the US. As of 2020, Billboard tallies *My Everything*'s sales at almost 760,000 copies, making it Ariana's best-selling album there.

Sometimes, making a sacrifice is worth it.

GEORGE GRIFFITHS

## 'PROBLEM' with Iggy Azalea

**Release date:** 28 April 2014
**Written by:** Ariana Grande, Iggy Azalea, Max Martin, Shellback, Ilya
**Produced by:** Max Martin, Shellback, Ilya, Peter Carlsson

Republic Records' Charlie Walk once waxed lyrical about a '30-second rule' for realising you have a hit song on your hands. As he tells it, 'You know the difference between good and great in 30 seconds.'[2]

With 'Problem', the star-making lead single from *My Everything*, I'd say it barely takes five. As soon as those saxophones play you in and you hear Ariana giggle, it's a party, it's a riot.

You would never know that launching Grande into 2014 with 'Problem' wasn't the original plan (she had been due to feature on a Chris Brown single, but that was pulled due to his many legal issues), but the song is so confident in its delivery and presentation of Ariana that it seems like it was the *only* option.

'Problem' is not just pop, it is *uber*-pop, straddling the realms of dance, bubblegum and hip-hop with alarming ease. It demands your attention, like all the best peacocking pop tracks do. Grande sounds *amazing* here, her voice mixed into the production and fitted like a glove. She sounds tough, yet soft. When her voice hits its apex, during the pre-chorus, it soars. She doesn't sound like

Ariana Grande doing a Mariah Carey impersonation anymore, she just sounds like Ariana Grande. Pure and simple. Plain and true.

A big part of 'Problem's success is the people Ariana chose to work with on the track. Chief among them Max Martin, a name you are likely to be aware of and a name you will be hearing a lot of for the rest of this book. Martin (real name Karl Martin Sandberg; the 'Max Martin' moniker was given to him by his mentor, the late producer Denniz Pop) is one of – if not *the* – best and most successful producers in all modern pop. I would reel off his CV for you here, but I have a word count to stick to! For clarity's sake, let's just leave it at that he's worked on career-defining projects for the likes of Britney Spears (. . . *Baby One More Time*), Katy Perry (*Teenage Dream*) and Taylor Swift (*1989*). Modern parlance goes that if you want a hit, you go to Martin and his cohorts in Sweden. In 2014, they found their newest muse in Grande.

Max Martin himself is notoriously publicity shy, but even he broke ranks after the release of 'Problem' to tell *Rolling Stone* that he worked with Ariana at the insistence of his daughter, no doubt a big *Victorious* fan.[3] One of his key beliefs as a producer is that there is a code to pop music and you need to crack it. Many of his collaborators have spoken about his 'melodic math', in the path, a dedication that sometimes disregards things like correct English grammar in pursuit of the purest, most addictive sound and melody a song can possess.

There is Swedish pop trickery aplenty in 'Problem'. The entire song starts at a high; the verses and pre-choruses have an urge and drive normally reserved for a song's chorus. However, *this* chorus drops out entirely, replaced with a melody little more than a whisper. The voice, uncredited on the track, belongs to rapper and Ariana's then-boyfriend, Big Sean. This was no accident. In a recent interview, co-writer Savan Kotecha confirmed that it was the intention from the start for 'Problem's structure to play with stereotypical pop expectations.[4]

The trick with 'Problem's chorus is especially effective – the song really *does* swell to bursting before it all suddenly disappears. It's a very intelligent take on the 'drop' that was prevalent in so many EDM songs at the time. In its own way, 'Problem' is quietly experimental, in the way that all the best Britney singles were back in their heyday. Chart-topping pop with bite, but you're having too much fun to realise all the work that's going on behind the curtain.

One thing 'Problem' was clearly crying out for is a feature and it was imperative that Grande found an MC who could cut a verse that matched the song's vivacious energy. Initially, she was mulling over reaching out to hip-hop duo the Ying Yang Twins, since 'Problem' takes explicit inspiration from their 2005 single, 'Wait (The Whisper Song)'.

As much as that would have been a nice nod to the track's heritage, Wendy Goldstein told *Rolling Stone* the duo tried to cut a verse but 'flopped it' so the next stop was clear: 'We figured [the feature] had to be a girl.'[5]

Enter Iggy Azalea.

Azalea told MTV that a big part of her accepting the verse on 'Problem' was the fact she got to work with Max Martin, who she had admired 'forever'. Martin even complimented her skills in the studio, saying she was an 'amazing' writer.[6] If Max Martin ever told *me* I was good at anything, I would never shut up about it. As usual, he was right too. Azalea's verse is just the right tempo for the song, bouncing on the beat, even if she *does* lose points for the too-obvious reference to Jay-Z's '99 Problems'.

It's unclear if Grande and Azalea worked directly in the studio together, but they *did* link up for the track's Mod-rock inspired music video, which leans heavily into the track's more muted vintage feel. It was probably a good thing to ease the transition from *Yours Truly* to *My Everything*, even if the visuals (directed once more by The Young Astronauts) hold no water in comparison to the song.

'Problem' was an immediate success, and a huge one at that. It shifted nearly half a million digital copies in its first week on sale in the US – debuting at Number 4 and eventually peaking at Number 2. Its path to the top spot, ironically, would be blocked by the artist Ariana had chosen to feature on the track. By this time, Iggy Azalea was on an all-time hot streak. After years of hard grind, she'd finally broken through. Her biggest hit,

'Fancy' with Charli xcx (another artist who had been hustling her way to the top for years and would continue to hustle for the next decade) had just become her first US Number 1 single. The song's seven weeks at the top of the Billboard Hot 100 were just too much for 'Problem' to overcome.

Honestly, though, don't be mad. Ariana may not have got to Number 1 here, and she would have a few years left to wait until she *did*, but no matter how much a chart-topper would have enshrined her as the pop girl of the moment, her eventual first Number 1 hit four years later would instead crown her an undeniable superstar. Good things come to those who wait.

'Problem' was the starting gun, the herald of great things to come. For some acts, a song *this* evocative would have been a near-impossible act to follow up. But one thing about the *My Everything* era? There was confidence to spare. It's no coincidence, then, that the next single from the record sounded nothing like 'Problem' . . . and was all the better for it.

ARIANA GRANDE

## 'BREAK FREE' with Zedd

**Release date:** 2 July 2014
**Written by:** Zedd, Max Martin, Savan Kotecha
**Produced by:** Zedd, Max Martin

Sometimes, all you need is a banger.

'Break Free', the second single from *My Everything*, is just that: a banger of *monstrous* proportions. It was a definite change in pace and tempo for the campaign and the point where Ariana Grande undeniably surrendered wholeheartedly to the pop machine.

'I never thought I'd do an EDM song,' she told *Billboard* before the single's official release in April 2014. 'But now all I want to do is dance.'[7] And dance she did.

Ariana is right: at the time, 'Break Free' was a totally different direction for her, but if you take the singles campaign for *My Everything* as a CV for everything she could do as a modern-day pop star, then 'Break Free' is the best example of her powers.

It's a towering electronic track, featuring the German DJ Zedd, who composed the song alongside Max Martin (him again!) and Savan Kotecha (the secret weapon during those formative years of turning Grande into an unbeatable commercial force, Kotecha seems like the glue that held together every record from *My Everything* to *Thank U, Next*, someone who really connected with the star on a creative level).

'Break Free' is brash and in your face. It hits you

right between the eyes. Lyrically, we're in breakup mode. Grande is getting up and she's getting over you – she's had enough! This is her chance to leave. To start a new life. To break free. The song's chorus, sung full-pelt and with total conviction, is probably the more life-affirming, foundational breakup text for teenagers since Kelly Clarkson's 'Since U Been Gone' (another Max Martin composition; I told you this man gets where water wouldn't). It's something that you scream at the top of your lungs when you've had enough, it's something to caption a particularly petty Facebook status in 2014 to signpost to people just how *over it* you are. Pop music is all about emotion, and there is emotion aplenty in 'Break Free'. It absolutely pores out of the speakers, like a geyser.

As you will no doubt notice, 'Break Free' also contains a featured artist, although you won't find their vocals anywhere on the track. Instead, this big, futuristic banger is a collaboration with the German DJ Zedd (real name Anton Zaslavski), who had only experienced his first true hit in the last two years, the hypnotic 'Clarity', which featured the British alt-pop vocalist Foxes. That song charted Top 10 in the US. Zedd clearly wanted to not just be known as an artist and DJ, but a hitmaking producer in his own right.

The track was supposedly originally intended for Austin Mahone, a social media star turned wannabe pop star in the early 2010s, although he was 'too busy' at the time to record it.[8] And so the song found its correct home. The best thing about 'Break Free' is how well Ariana's towering vocals match the cascading ripples of its hard-edged production. You need to be a *vocalist* to pull it off. Grande and Zedd have never worked together again and she has never really committed so heavily to a dance-pop aesthetic again on one of her own projects. It remains a fascinating diversion for her.

'Nobody really expected this to become this anthem,' Zedd said around the song's tenth anniversary in 2024. 'It's [still] one of the biggest songs in my sets. It certainly wouldn't have happened without [Grande]. She drove that thing home.'[9]

One of the most interesting stories around 'Break Free' is pretty enlightening into the mind of the great pop genius himself, Max Martin. As a Swede, Martin's first language naturally isn't English and as I mentioned before, the way he approaches composing a song is much the same way as you would solve a puzzle: he looks at the pieces and judges where to place them for the best fit. Sometimes this means ignoring something as simple as basic grammar to engineer the best melody possible. A good example of this is probably Martin's biggest hit with the Backstreet Boys, 'I Want It That Way'. Please read the lyrics to that song and tell me what it's actually about – you can't! Something similar is at work on 'Break Free' and recently, Grande herself revealed a specific annoyance she had when recording the song with Martin.

'I was a lot younger [when I recorded 'Break Free'],' she told the popular online show *Hot Ones*.[10] 'I did *not* want to do the intonation on *sayidontwantcha* [during the song's chorus].'

Apparently, Martin was insistent it *had* to sound that way, in Grande's own words 'pingy and annoying', for it to work. She reluctantly relented and that vocal cut is what made it onto the record. Sometimes, you just have to listen to the greats!

Also, it would be remiss of me not to mention the video to 'Break Free' because it is absolutely bonkers. It's Grande by way of *Star Wars* and *Flash Gordon*. It's space but through the filter of 1950s pulp science fiction. The story is somewhat incoherent. Grande is a space trooper. Or assassin? Or soldier of some kind? It's never clear. Anyway! She gets kidnapped by a robot and kills Ming the Merciless in a volcano pit. But that's not the point. The clip, directed by Chris Marrs Piliero, is reminiscent of some of Katy Perry's best kitschy offerings during the *Teenage Dream* era. There also seems to be a specific callback to the 'California Gurls' music video, where Perry straps whipped cream canisters to her bra and lets rip. Because while there's no whipped cream in sight in the 'Break Free' visual, Grande's bra *does* replace her actual breasts with rockets when fighting a robot foe.

Probably my favourite live clip of Grande comes from her performing 'Break Free' at an iHeart Radio showcase not long after the song's release in 2014. The stage's set is made up to look like its retro-futuristic music video, Ariana has a fresh spray tan, a new balayage and a crisp white microphone stained with her cherry-pink lipstick.

She performs the track with absolute aplomb, jumping up and down in sky-high platform stiletto boots while not missing a single beat. 'Break Free' is not an easy song to sing live, especially with choreography; it's frantic and loud and you have to both keep up with the tempo and the track's skyscraper high adlibs. Grande is clearly fighting for her life, but she pulls it off. I'm always in awe of it, every time I watch it. It's certainly not her most accomplished live performance ever, but this is what a *real* pop star looks like, ladies and gentlemen.

That is exactly what 'Break Free' is – Grande bursting out of her cocoon as a fully formed pop star, rocket bra at the ready, ready to conquer not just the world, but the whole galaxy.

## 'BANG BANG' with Jessie J and Nicki Minaj

**Release date:** 28 July 2014
**Written by:** Max Martin, Ariana Grande, Nicki Minaj, Savan Kotecha, Rickard Göransson
**Produced by:** Max Martin, Rickard Göransson, Ilya

The origins of 'Bang Bang' — the closest the current pop generation has come to remaking the all-star team-up of 'Lady Marmalade' — are fraught.

According to Jessie J, 'Bang Bang' was recorded first by her, before its producer, Max Martin, requested the presence of Ariana Grande on it. But according to Republic Records A&R head Wendy Goldstein (both Grande and Jessie J were signed to Republic at the time, though Jessie has since left), Ariana had originally demoed the track during sessions for *My Everything* before abandoning it. 'She hated it,' Goldstein told *Billboard*, revealing the singer only agreed to record her verse after hearing a new version with both Jessie J and superstar rapper Nicki Minaj.[11]

So, the question is . . . why did Ariana hate 'Bang Bang' so much?

Well, you have to give it to her. It is very loud. So loud, in fact, that it veers closely into camp territory at times. As vocalists, Jessie J and Grande are noted for their considerable reach, but they don't sound in harmony here. They basically spend three minutes screaming at each other, with enough volume between them to break glass or alert every dog within a 25-mile vicinity.

The only thing with enough power to bring these two warring nations together turns out to be a verse from Nicki Minaj herself. She blasts through without pausing for breath and manages to namedrop Batman and Robin, the American folktale *The Little Engine That Could*, both artists she's working with *and* her own-brand wine in less than a minute.

You also have to feel sorry for poor Jessie J. After scoring three UK Number 1 singles from her debut album, *Who You Are* (all three of those tracks, 'Do It Like A Dude', 'Price Tag' and 'Domino' are brilliant, even if they hold no cohesion together, which was Jessie's big problem artistically) but her second album, *Alive*, felt like a retread of past glories and she was badly in need of a win. This was supposed to be a *hit*, her big breakout moment in the US, but she's clearly not the star of the show here. Even kept shuttered away in the song's second verse, this is Ariana Grande's show. The single became a Top 10 hit in the US, peaking at Number 3; it also topped the charts in the UK, becoming Grande's second Number 1 there, after 'Problem'. So much of the track's popularity was due to Ariana's star being in absolute ascent during its release. Jessie J hasn't had another Top 10 hit in either the US or the UK.

'Bang Bang's big issue is that it really doesn't *feel* like an Ariana Grande song. You can certainly see why she passed on it at first; it sounds way too similar to 'Problem' to stick out in any meaningful way. Also, clearly no one was available for a photoshoot for the single cover, so they just took three separate press photos and thought, 'that'll do!', which shows how limited the marketing emphasis was on this track. It was clearly going to be a big hit, and the link-up felt impressive and of-the-moment, but 'Bang Bang' just feels empty and hollow. A victory for no one in particular. I can't remember the last time Grande played it live, for instance, which shows you its diminished legacy in her discography.

Still, we'll always have Nicki's verse.

ARIANA GRANDE

# 'LOVE ME HARDER' with The Weeknd

**Release date:** 30 September 2014
**Written by:** Max Martin, The Weeknd, Belly, Savan Kotecha, Ali Payami, Peter Svensson
**Produced by:** Ali Payami, Peter Svensson

Sex, and sexuality, are hard things to get right. *Especially* for former child stars. Shy away from them and pretend they don't exist, you'll essentially become frozen in amber as a teenager. Go *too* hard in the other direction and the gap between your former image and now growing adulthood can become disruptive.

Miley Cyrus, who felt that disruption better than any other during 2013's *Bangerz* has said it best of her controversial image change.

'What I did wasn't shocking,' the former *Hannah Montana* star told *Billboard*. 'It was who I *was* that was shocking.'[12]

Ariana Grande would be more interested in expanding on sex and her sexuality in later albums, but her greatest contribution to the 'pop songs about sex' canon might just come in the form of 'Love Me Harder', a rare moment when two future superstars met on a record just before they both exploded into the stratosphere. It's a classic case of two artists that on paper wouldn't seem to make much sense on the same track but put them together and that contrasting mismatch proves to make unexpected magic.

'Love Me Harder' is a lesson in restraint. It's not the most outwardly sexual song Grande has ever put her name to, but it could well be her most sensual. Its relationship to sex is the same as all the great Janet Jackson records, one where the act itself is just off-screen. All we see is the build-up of indescribable longing before the explosion takes place.

The Weeknd was an artist familiar with the art of indescribable longing. He had started 2014 critically adored and with an ever-growing fanbase, but wanted to break out of the blogs and into the Top 10. Debut LP *Kiss Land* proved that he didn't have the cultural capital to do that on his own, so he would need a little help along the way. Luckily, both The Weeknd and Ariana Grande are signed to Republic Records and he was invited to cut a verse on the track by Republic Records' VP Charlie Walk, who said it was 'no accident' that he was the featured guest on the track. He told *Hits Double Daily*, '[It was] strategic. He's about to blow up with his own record.'[13]

It may have been major-label machinations that brought them together in the first place, but Ariana Grande and The Weeknd are an inspired pairing and it's no mistake they've continued to collaborate in the years since 'Love Me Harder'. On the track, they bring contrasting shades of light and dark, Grande hesitant yet wanting, The Weeknd clear-eyed and tempting. The production of the track – helmed by Wolf Cousins members Ali Payami and former The Cardigans member

Peter Svensson – pulsates like the beating of a heart in the midnight shadows.

The trick worked. Savan Kotecha confirmed in a 2024 interview that The Weeknd was hungry for more chart-friendly material and the match-up with Max Martin and co. on 'Love Me Harder' showed him the way forward. This would be the first of many tracks he would work on with Wolf Cousins. In fact, just the next year, in 2015, The Weeknd would hold a coming-out party as a pop star in his own right with the scorching-hot 'Can't Feel My Face', written and produced, naturally, by Max Martin and co.[14]

A decade on from its release the track stands up. It's also important to contextualise this as the start of a long-running and seriously beneficial partnership between the two artists. Their initial meeting may have been engineered for optimum success, but the pair found each other to be kindred spirits. The Weeknd would call on Grande to help him remix two of his album tracks to become Number 1 hits, while he would return the favour as a featured artist on one of the spikier cuts from 2020's *Positions*, a much more grown-up take on sex and sexuality than anything we've seen here.

'Love Me Harder' would become The Weeknd's first-ever US Top 10 hit single. His all-time tally now stands at twenty, including seven Number 1s, two of them with Grande – and don't worry, we'll get to those!

*My Everything* had confidently built upon the foundations that *Yours Truly* had laid, transforming Ariana

Grande from a wannabe ingénue into one of the most in-demand and famous women on the planet. Of course, all this happened within the span of twelve months, so it's no surprise to hear that she found her sudden ascent to superstardom difficult to deal with.

'One minute I was Cat Valentine,' she recalled of that time, 'and the next I was singing R&B and making out with Mac Miller.'[15] Grande herself admitted that 'becoming a pop star at nineteen, twenty is insane,' even going so far as to tell *Hot Ones* that she struggled, in the years after her debut, to connect with the material she was making at this time.

'There was a time when it was hard for me to feel the gratitude I do now for certain songs. But with time and therapy, we sort of are able to re-embrace, so I feel just really proud and grateful and happy when I hear them. I'm like, "That's a good song." Whereas I used to maybe hear it and cry.'[16]

Whatever her feelings on the era, it's hard not to see that stardom was well earned. She had made smart choices with the singles she'd released, building up a persona that was more nuanced than simply 'Ariana Grande sounds a bit like Mariah Carey'.

Now, Grande had topped the charts, collaborated with some of the most exciting new voices in commercial music and even as *My Everything*'s promo trail came to an end, there was still excitement in the air. Why? Because you knew that she was just getting started.

The doors were left wide open for her return, and

there was no doubt about it: she was on the cusp of being a superstar. All she needed was the material to get there.

GEORGE GRIFFITHS

## 'SANTA TELL ME'

**Release date:** 24 November 2014
**Written by:** Ariana Grande, Savan Kotecha, Ilya
**Produced by:** Ilya

Not everyone has an original Christmas song that is actually good. It probably didn't *seem* like it at the time, but this one-off release from Ariana Grande has in the last decade grown in festive stature so much that I'm convinced in the next ten years we'll be calling 'Santa Tell Me' the new 'All I Want For Christmas Is You', one of the rare modern festive songs to enter the all-time holiday canon.

The funny thing about 'Santa Tell Me' is that its story feels like it hasn't even really begun yet — it's still on the rise. When it was first released, Grande was an old hat at cashing in on the Christmas market. Just before the promo trail for *My Everything* had begun, she'd released a Christmas EP, *Christmas Kisses*, once again working with *Yours Truly* producer Harmony Samuels. *Christmas Kisses* is fine but there was a sense of fun and play and dare I say it *joie de Noël* missing.

That would soon be rectified with 'Santa Tell Me', sweet as a candy cane and just as likely to leave you with an intense sugar rush. It's a silly, frilly song that pulls off its pastiche very well but, like the best Christmas songs, it's *more* than pastiche. It communicates something about the most wonderful time of year, like all the great holiday standards do; namely, that you do not want to be alone at Christmas, and you do not want the magic to fade. The most important part of any Christmas song is that it needs to make you believe in magic – and Santa Claus – again. That you can listen to those songs when you are four, twenty-four and sixty-four and still get the same reaction. That Christmas is coming around once again and you can't wait to open your presents and spend time with your loved ones.

It's easy to make a Christmas song; what's hard is making a *good* one. One that can stand the test of time. 'Last Christmas' and 'All I Want For Christmas Is You' are classics for a reason, but the path to them is littered with similar festive fare by similarly big (if not bigger) names that also tried to put their own stamp on the holidays and receive those big, fat royalty checks down the chimney each December, of course. But not everyone can be Wham! or Mariah Carey. Could you name Katy Perry or Lady Gaga's original Christmas songs? Quickly? I didn't think so. It's a hard job – harder than it seems – and your chances of long-lasting success are slim. You just have to go for it.

Ariana Grande went for it. She approaches greatness with a swing in her step on 'Santa Tell Me'. Why is that? I don't really know. The track was recorded and released during the dying days of *My Everything*'s 2014 campaign, the blitzkrieg of promotional appearances and single drops that had transformed her career forever. Maybe it was through all this chaos and noise that she was able to channel the Christmas spirit. Maybe it gave her respite, or perhaps inspiration struck just when she was busiest.

Either way, releasing an original Christmas song isn't most people's number-one priority when they've just had the busiest and most successful year of their professional life. But Ariana Grande has never been one to stick by tradition and her punt with 'Santa Tell Me' has paid off in the long run. Above all else, pop music is about longevity, make no mistake about it.

The 'Santa Tell Me' video isn't quite as timeless. I don't know what about rolling around in a bedroom in your vaguely festive pyjamas when it's probably a scorching-hot LA day outside says 'Christmas' but that's what was created! In an interview accepting several billion stream plaques for Spotify, Grande revealed that her initial idea for 'Santa Tell Me's music video was a bit more risqué.

'[In the original video that was filmed] I was [dressed] in weird Christmas lingerie,' she said.[17] 'I was hitting Santa with a cane pole. It was something I was really insistent on.'

Insistent she might have been, but her label balked at the original cut and we ended up with the video we have, shot on the fly with no real budget.

With a modern Christmas song, you can't expect instant results. Even 'Last Christmas' and 'All I Want For Christmas Is You' took decades to really take hold with the public's imagination. Though, when first released, 'Santa Tell Me' did decently enough. During its original chart run in the US, it peaked at Number 42, but over the years 'Santa Tell Me' has grown in esteem (and streams!), entering the US Top 40 for the first time in 2020, before finally reaching the Top 10, and eventually Top 5 in 2024, peaking at Number 5. It's all-time tally now stands at over a billion streams on Spotify, a number that is surely to rise each festive season. In 2024, Spotify named it as the most-streamed Christmas song to come from the modern era.[18]

It's within reason that, in the next five years, we could see it go all the way to Number 1. What a Christmas present that would be!

# 4
# *Dangerous Woman* – A Career-shifting Statement

The way Ariana Grande chose to describe *Dangerous Woman*, her third – and at that point, most ambitious – album is, I think, pretty spot on.

'A 22-year-old girl comes into her own trying to balance growing up, love and a lot of other bullshit along the way.'[1]

Levelling up as a pop star is hard. So hard, in fact, that some never manage it. It's not just a tricky balancing act, it can be deadly. A tightrope walk between two skyscrapers, with nothing but air below you, should you fall. The key to pulling it off is confidence and vision. On her third album, Ariana Grande had both of those things in spades.

*Dangerous Woman* is a bold name for a bold record. It attempts to do numerous things – recontextualise Grande's place in the apex of the pop pantheon, help mature her as an artist and combine the disparate styles of her first two albums into one cohesive whole – and does them all incredibly well. It's not *perfect*, but it's her first definitive statement as an artist in her own right. Plus, it has 'Into You' – her best song ever – on the track list. That must count for something, surely!

But the path to *Dangerous Woman* was not an easy one. When work first started on the album, it wasn't even supposed to be *called* that. Much like after the release of her first album, while Ariana was on tour for *My Everything*, she was already thinking about what her next era would sound like.

'I feel like I'm just getting started,' she said at the time. 'A lot of people forget I'm only three years in [to my pop career].'² Speed is the name of the game in fighting to the top of the pop pyramid. *Yours Truly* and *My Everything* had arrived within a twelve-month span of each other and it looked like she was about to repeat that trick for a third time.

During initial sessions with Victoria Monét and Tommy Brown, Grande's third album was created with the title *Moonlight* in mind. Work, it seemed, was happening quickly.

'I'm really happy with what we've done so far,' she told UK radio station KISS FM in the summer of 2015. 'I'm going to maybe outdo what we've already done. *Maybe*.'

While there was no music immediately, Ariana started branching out from just releasing pop bangers. She hadn't acted since her *Victorious* spin-off, *Sam & Cat*, had been cancelled after just one season, mostly due to the singer's ascendant career – she didn't have the time to release albums *and* record dozens of sitcom episodes! She did, however, find an outlet to flex her acting muscles, joining the cast of Ryan Murphy's highly underrated teen slasher drama *Scream Queens* (2015). Her presence in the show – as a character called Chanel Number 2, an underling of Emma Roberts' catty lead Chanel Oberlin – was a bit of a fake-out. She took the Drew Barrymore role of the famous cast member unceremoniously killed off in the opening episode. Watch her death scene, it's great. She spends so much time Tweeting that she's about to be killed that she, uh, gets killed. Satire!

But music remained her main priority. The looming third album was important; Grande wanted to grow up and level up. While 2015 wouldn't see an album release, it *would* bring one of the hallmarks of any celebrity's growing career – her first scandal. At the time, she had broken off her eight-month courtship with Big Sean and entered a relationship with Ricky Alvarez, who had been employed as a dancer on her Honeymoon Tour in support of *Yours Truly*.

We've mentioned before now that Ariana's growing celebrity status had seen her relationship with Big Sean become tabloid fodder but her relationship with Alvarez would contain another first for Grande – her first major scandal.

In July 2015, they had stopped off for a late-night visit to a donut shop, where CCTV footage captured Grande licking donuts that had been placed on display, while giggling and stating, 'I hate Americans. I hate America. This is disgusting.'

The backlash was swift and consistent, and Grande apologised in no uncertain terms, stating that she 'loved' being an American and her words had been taken out of context – she had been referring to the obesity epidemic in the US.

Maybe if this had happened during the current era – where 'cancel culture' is a lot more prevalent – the scandal would have stuck, but thankfully for Grande and donut lovers everywhere, it didn't. It wasn't a great look, for sure, but *everyone* has to have a scandal at some point in their career and the backlash that ensued wasn't enough to define Grande or her persona, as had been the case for Miley Cyrus just a few years earlier, for example.

As 2015 drew to a close, we got the first taste of what *Moonlight* would sound like with its lead single, 'Focus'. It was an exuberantly produced Max Martin affair, no doubt about it, but too much of the song sounded similar to 'Problem'. Almost *too* similar – 'Focus' employs a similar trick in its chorus, with an uncredited Jamie Foxx whispering the song's hook.

It was for the best, then, that *Moonlight* never appeared after 'Focus's release. In fact, we heard no more about the tentative release of Grande's third album until the new year, when she announced on *The Tonight Show Starring Jimmy Fallon* that work on the album had now been completed. More than that, though, the album wasn't called *Moonlight* at all, but *Dangerous Woman*.

'*Moonlight* is a lovely song and a lovely title,' Ariana told fans in an online meet-up before the LP's release. 'But *Dangerous Woman* is a lot stronger. My personal growth is reflected in the sound. I'm really proud of it.'³

She's not wrong. Some days, I think *Dangerous Woman* might be my favourite Ariana Grande album. It's certainly the one I revisit most often. The record's central conceit is Grande's attempt to combine the work of her two favoured collaborators at this point in her career: Tommy Brown and Max Martin. Both seem to intuitively understand her as an artist, but their styles are contrasting. Brown favours R&B stylings with a more low-slung feel, while Martin's work embraces full-bodied pop. Would there be a way for her to work with these two sides of her identity? The stylings that had defined the two albums she had released so far, and to be able to find a way forward?

The answer on *Dangerous Woman* is yes. It's a balancing act, of course, but one that Grande pulls off with relative ease. In the hands of another pop star, perhaps, you would see the gaps between her work with Brown and Martin more heavily. But not here. The two sides work in tandem with each other, building the world of the album around the conceit of confidence in stepping into herself as a woman.

You can see this just by looking at its cover. Cast in shades of black and white, we can see Ariana from the neck up; she wears an ornate diamond necklace and, more fetching still, a black latex mask fixed with bunny ears. It's a striking, sensual update from the cat ears that she had sported throughout *My Everything*.

It also tells you more about the persona she's channelling for this record. Heavily inspired by film noir, you could say that Grande on the cover of *Dangerous Woman* is part femme fatale, part bank robber – if you robbed banks in stiletto heels and latex rabbit ears, of course.

*Dangerous Woman* is a record about growth, it's about finding yourself – more so than the scattershot references to relationships, love and breakups in *My Everything*, this feels for the first time like Grande pulling from her own life in her material. She starts talking about sex seriously and about the dichotomy between feeling more confident in yourself as you grow up, yet less confident in the relationships you have with those around you. Some of these relationships are destructive ('Bad Decisions', 'Sometimes'), some of them are melancholic ('Moonlight', 'Be Alright') and some are yet unfulfilled, but cresting towards a climax ('Into You', 'Thinking Bout You').

It's an ambitious record, full of confidence and smart decisions, whether on a lyrical or sonic level. This, for perhaps the first time, felt like an Ariana Grande album made by, and for, Ariana Grande.

The dichotomy at the heart of the first decade of Grande's career has been the gentle and steady push-and-pull between commercial success and personal gratification. *Dangerous Woman* was the start of one receding to the other before both met in the middle, directed by the gravity of a true, undeniable star.

*Dangerous Woman* sounded and felt like the record of an artist who was ready to be a superstar. But despite the undeniable confidence and ambition contained in this work, this metamorphosis was somewhat stymied. It was Ariana's first (and, so far, only) album to miss Number 1 in the US, instead being held off by Drake's blockbuster *Views*, which had been bolstered by the massive success of watercooler singles like 'Hotline Bling' and 'One Dance'. At this time Drake was the undeniable superstar of pop and his release schedule would inspire Ariana Grande's own true ascent to A-list pop act not three years later.

The title track continued her unbeaten record of lead singles debuting inside the Top 10, but that pesky Number 1 single still avoided her and I know we all let out a sizeable groan of defeat when 'Into You' didn't become the world-mauling hit it so clearly deserved to be.

Still, Grande may not have jumped up another level, but she was still comfortable where she was, and she was clearly enamoured with the material she had pulled together. The release of the album saw the launch of her biggest tour yet. The Dangerous Woman Tour stretched across the US, UK, Europe, Latin America, Asia, Australia and New Zealand. It was her most ambitious live tour to date. At best, it was the celebration of an album that had begun to mould Ariana Grande into a new woman, and a better artist.

GEORGE GRIFFITHS

## 'DANGEROUS WOMAN'

**Release date:** 11 March 2016
**Written by:** Ross Golan, Johan Carlsson, Max Martin
**Produced by:** Max Martin, Johan Carlsson

If you ever wondered what it would sound like if Ariana Grande recorded a James Bond theme, then look no further! 'Dangerous Woman' earns its stripes as the title track of Grande's pivotal third album and, I would argue, one of the most important singles of her career. It was here that Ariana Grande started to become *Ariana Grande*. Which is incredibly ironic, considering that not only was she not involved in the writing or production of this song, but it wasn't even written for her in the first place.

To dive into the genesis of 'Dangerous Woman', we need to go back to one of its co-writers, the US songwriter Ross Golan (who has worked with the likes of Selena Gomez, Sabrina Carpenter and Charlie Puth – who is credited with beatboxing on 'Dangerous Woman'!). The bare bones of what would become one of the most pivotal singles of Grande's career started as a reference track to pitch to former *American Idol* winner, Carrie Underwood.

According to Golan, he originally brought his demo of 'Dangerous Woman' to Johan Carlsson (a member of Wolf Cousins, which explains Martin's later presence on the track as a co-writer and producer; artists like Selena

Gomez and Taylor Swift have in the past spoken about Martin entering the process only when he feels like he has something to add or enhance when a song is being worked on) and his initial idea for the track lent more country, explaining why his first idea was to pitch it to Underwood, who had firmly entrenched herself in the genre following her *American Idol* victory of 2005.

Whether 'Dangerous Woman' ever made its way into the hands of Underwood is unclear (she's never spoken about it on the record anywhere and maybe she's even unaware of the song's genesis in the first place), but before Ariana Grande cut it, Golan told US chat show *CBS This Morning* that he'd also considered sending the song to Alicia Keys and, of course, Rihanna. But, according to Golan, it was Grande who clinched the song, walking into the session and saying, 'If [you let me release 'Dangerous Woman'], I promise to treat it well.'[4]

Treat it well she did – with the track obviously serving as potent inspiration for both her third album and her worldwide tour. While it would have been great to hear Rihanna's take on 'Dangerous Woman', I like to think the track found its perfect home in Grande.

To compare 'Dangerous Woman' to, say, 'Problem', is like trying to compare the dark with the light. 'Problem' was the sound of someone who was trying to make a hit. 'Dangerous Woman' chugs along, defying your expectations of what an Ariana Grande song could sound like – because she had never sounded like *this*.

'I feel like people are always constantly trying to

pin me down as a good girl or a bad girl,' Grande told *Grazia*. 'But I think women can be whatever, and me too.'³

You can hear this fight to reclaim her identity on 'Dangerous Woman', whose percussion is based around a dirty and deep guitar riff worth noting because of what it's trying to get across to the listener. This is a serious moment; this is an Ariana Grande they had never encountered before. Gone was the pop princess with the cat ears and the rocket bra, here was a femme fatale with a cigarette holder in-between her lips and a smoking gun between perfectly manicured fingers.

'Dangerous Woman' is the sound of Grande evolving in front of us in real time. She had never recorded a song like this before, and she's never really recorded one like it since. I think that's for a reason. As a starting gun, and a handy do-over, for her third era, you could do no better. It's not just a reintroduction, it's a re-casting. Sex, something we know that Grande shied away from confronting head-on in her first two albums, is here. It's at the centre of the song, in fact, although like all the best film noir, it's dressed up in the subtext, covered in the smoke and chaos of a speakeasy at 2 a.m.

'I want it to be strong and empowering because I've come into my own a little bit,' Grande told Ryan Seacrest. 'Whereas before, I think I was afraid to be myself and make decisions and speak out about things I'm passionate about because I thought it would make me experience some of the stereotypes that women in power often face.'

When talking to Jimmy Kimmel about the scrapping of the *Moonlight* concept, Grande admitted that recording 'Dangerous Woman' 'changed everything' about her third album. You can hear it here, Ariana stepping into herself in real time.[6]

Front and centre, of course, is Grande's most powerful tool – her voice. And my God, does she put it to use here! A rarity at this time in her career, her timbre is brought down to a husk, only exploding into the skyscraper-high diva adlibs as the song draws to a close. She talks candidly about not just stepping into sex and sexuality, but owning it. Dominating it. There's a reason why the song's full-pelt arena rock chorus, perhaps the best James Bond theme never released, is a pleasing twist on Aretha Franklin's 'You Make Me Feel (Like A Natural Woman)'. This is natural, but it's also dangerous – and there's nothing a femme fatale loves more than danger.

If you were in doubt that 'Dangerous Woman' was the beginning of a bold new era for Grande, then just look at the track's lo-fi music video. Directed by The Young Astronauts, the visual looks like it's filmed through old-fashioned video cameras, with Ariana decked out in black lingerie, crooning in a bedroom. The most important statement of the entire thing? That she's let her signature high ponytail go, her hair falls full and wavy down her body. The pop star persona has cracked, if only for a second, and she's letting you see the real her – the real dangerous woman.

Sadly, though, there is one 'Dangerous Woman' video we will never get to see. When the original video was launched, it was pinned with the intention to release a second visual, but that twin release never came to fruition.

In a since-deleted fan Q&A on Snapchat, Ariana confirmed that the second video was scrapped due to timing and effects work. Apparently, the video would have seen her strip off her own skin (!) to reveal the leather bunny mask she wears on the album's cover. Perhaps wise to leave that one on the cutting-room floor.[7]

'Dangerous Woman' was a bold choice to start a new era with. It wasn't as maximalist or full-on pop as 'Problem', but if Grande was sweating, she never admitted to it. Instead, the single performed well, if not the world-ending gangbusters that maybe everyone was hoping this sharp but subtle reintroduction would pull off.

In the US, 'Dangerous Woman' debuted at Number 10 (another extension of that record of each album's lead single debuting inside the Top 10), before reaching a brand-new peak of Number 8 during its eleventh week on the chart. In 2021, RIAA (Recording Industry Association of America) classified 'Dangerous Woman' as a 4x platinum record, constituting sales of 4 million in the US.[8]

But something bigger was on the horizon. As the release date of the new album loomed, Ariana would re-share a story on her Instagram, showing her mother, Joan, reacting to 'Dangerous Woman'.

'That,' she says, almost breathless, 'is the best song I have ever heard.'

## 'INTO YOU'

**Release date:** 6 May 2016
**Written by:** Ariana Grande, Max Martin, Ilya, Savan Kotecha, Alexander Kronlund
**Produced by:** Max Martin, Ilya

How do you think an artist feels when they know they've made a masterpiece? The defining work of their career?

When ABBA left the studio after recording 'Dancing Queen', or Madonna listened to the final cut of 'Like A Prayer', was there a sense of relief in the air? Euphoria, perhaps? Or maybe there was just a cool, serene calm. Nothing is more reassuring than the realisation that you've finally hit upon *it* – the kind of pop nirvana that most artists only ever dream of entering.

This is now a direct call-out to Ariana Grande: please tell me how you felt when you finished 'Into You' for the first time. Did you know then that you had just created one of the best pop songs of the twenty-first century? I'm pretty sure you did. How could you not?

'Into You' is, by some margin and to my ears at least, the best song Grande has ever put her name to. It takes everything she had learnt under the tutelage of Max Martin – how to control her voice, how to emote, how to construct a chorus and a post-chorus – and perfects it. 'Into You' is the endgame. It was the ultimate sign that one part of her career had come to an end and another one was just beginning. It's one of those songs that is entirely indicative. I'm pretty sure, in practice, that 'Into You' could feasibly have been given to any one of Max Martin's muses at the time – Taylor Swift, Ellie Goulding, or even Katy Perry – but no one could have pulled it off quite like Ariana Grande.

She wanted, *needed*, to communicate something through 'Into You'. She found the perfect vessel through which to preach her sermon of growth and maturity.

'Into You' is a song about desire. A desire that, in the moment, is so all-encompassing, it threatens to consume you entirely. The scene is set thus: Grande wants to get closer to her partner. She is *so* into him that she can barely breathe and she wants to know that the feeling is mutual. The entire song is built around this conceit; of a love and attraction so strong, it threatens to pull the world off its axis. It may just be for one night, or it could be for life, but right now, in the moment, it is everything . . . and she doesn't want to let it go.

The production of this song feels full enough to straddle entire galaxies. It's built over a throbbing club beat, backed with synthesised moaning that only adds to the intensity of the whole thing. It's electronic, certainly, but as the track blooms with each passing second, it becomes more than simply a club cut. There are sharp clicks intonating Grande's growing frustration, they sound like heels walking over broken glass. The chorus – oh, that chorus – explodes with flavours of post-disco funk, like Daft Punk had suddenly decided to throw a midnight rave on the moon. It's maximalist in the way that other Martin productions for Grande – like 'Problem' and 'Break Free' especially – were, but there's more emotion and intent piled into the music and lyrics. The synthesisers and the drums, the clicks and the murmurs all work in tandem with the song's greatest strength: Grande's vocal performance. She's as slick and cool as ice on the verses, cooing about her desire for her partner – she *wants* to cross the line within him, she senses the danger but she wants more. A sense of anticipation is in the air, building. Getting hotter. Who's going to make the first move?

'Dangerous Woman' re-cast Ariana Grande as a sensual femme fatale for her brand era and 'Into You' sends her, spiralling, into the club. Right into the heat of the moment. That's when the chorus explodes. Because if the verses are a lesson in restraint then the chorus is in giving into your desires. Ariana tells you what she wants, and how she wants it. She references both 'A Little Less Conversation' by Elvis Presley and 'Touch My Body' by Mariah Carey in the same line as the drums begin to bounce off the walls.

Things slow down for the song's bridge; where 'Into You' begins to dissect itself, a few key lines repeating into the ether, before Grande prepares for one last go-around. It's only then, during the last chorus, that Martin and Ilya really let her vocals fly. It's the first and final hint that, by the song's end, Ariana and her partner have let their desire consume them, whole.

I hope you have a re-listen of 'Into You' after you've

read this, and I hope during your listening session you think, wow, this song is great, it sounds like a Number 1 single. Well, yes! But somehow, it wasn't!

If you were an Ariana Grande fan, then watching 'Into You' climb the charts in 2016 was akin to being a general drafting up plans the night before a big battle. It seemed almost inconceivable that the song wouldn't succeed, but it just wasn't meant to be. 'Into You' peaked at Number 13 in the US – *just* missing the Top 10, yes, but still a disappointing result for a single that seemed primed to send Grande rocketing into pop's A-list.

So, why wasn't this a gigantic worldwide hit? One theory would be due to timing. The year 2016 was a year in which rap music dominated the conversation and airwaves, with hits like Drake's aforementioned 'One Dance' and Rae Sremmurd and Gucci Mane's 'Black Beatles' soaring, and 'Into You' was simply just too pop to cut through the noise. It was too sleek and produced, and it was released into the world where the listening public's instincts were growing towards needing more 'authenticity' from their favourite artists. It's no coincidence that in the next few years, we would see the rise of artists like Billie Eilish, whose authenticity is baked into her pop persona. Or, indeed, that Grande herself would begin to make more authentic music and then experience the biggest commercial successes of her career.

'Into You', for however undoubtedly great it is, is not so achingly honest as songs to come. It *does* feel authentic to where Grande was in her career at this point – and her attempts to grow up, both artistically and personally – but lyrically, it doesn't feel ripped out of the pages of her diary.

Nearly ten years on from the original release, 'Into You' stands tall in the hallowed halls of Ariana Grande's discography. Indie gatekeepers *Pitchfork* named it as one of the Top 100 best songs of 2016,[9] while in recent years *Billboard*, the *Guardian* and *Rolling Stone* have all described it as the best song of Grande's career.

The praise doesn't just stop with the critics, either. 'Into You' now ranks as Ariana's fifth most-streamed song ever on Spotify, with 1.7 billion streams at the time of writing. And if *all that* isn't enough to convince you, beloved indie pop goddess Lorde once waxed lyrical on the brilliance of 'Into You', comparing it to similarly overlooked pop gem 'Run Away With Me' by Carly Rae Jepsen.

'People weren't truly ready to comprehend that many layers of emotion,' Lorde wrote. 'It's too much for the half-open heart.'[10]

ARIANA GRANDE

## 'SIDE TO SIDE' with Nicki Minaj

**Release date:** 30 August 2016
**Written by:** Ariana Grande, Nicki Minaj, Max Martin, Ilya, Savan Kotecha, Alexander Kronlund
**Produced by:** Max Martin, Ilya

Remember what I said about 'Love Me Harder' being a lesson in restraint? Less is more when it comes to signposting sex in your pop songs. Well, 'Side To Side' is the opposite of that. It's loud and brash and although built around something of a double entendre, it doesn't take much to work out what Ariana Grande is *actually* singing about here.

When asked by *Vogue* in 2019 about whether she ever felt uncomfortable about releasing 'Side To Side' as a single, or performing it on tour, in front of her young fans, Grande was refreshingly unapologetic.

'They're for sure gonna have [sex one day]. I promise that your kid's gonna have sex,' she says, directing herself to any parents in the audience at her shows. 'So if [your child] asks you what the song's about, talk about it!'[11]

'Side To Side' may not rank too highly in the hallowed halls of Ariana Grande's best singles, but it certainly got the job done, becoming the biggest hit of the *Dangerous Woman* era by quite some margin. It's just a shame that, for a record so concerned with levelling up Ariana's craft, this seems oddly juvenile.

Let's start with the obvious elephant in the room.

'Side To Side' is, explicitly, about the act of having sex. In fact, you're having so much sex that the next morning, you find yourself walking funny. Side to side, if you will. Look, no one said it was the demurest metaphor in the world!

The most interesting thing about 'Side To Side' is that it, again, sounds completely different to what came before. 'Dangerous Woman' was an arena-rock jam, 'Into You' a scintillating electronic-club banger, while 'Side To Side' mostly plays about in the genres of reggae and dancehall.

In 2016, dancehall was having a moment. It was the reference point for two of the biggest hits of that year: Drake's 'One Dance' (although I would also argue 'One Dance' is just as much an Afrobeats track) and Rihanna's 'Work'. Both Number 1 hits were significant; Drake used 'One Dance' to help proclaim him as the most invulnerable of modern-day hitmakers. It was, for a time, the most-streamed song in Spotify history, although Drake's bulletproof hitmaker status would collapse dramatically when Kendrick Lamar had something to say in 2024. For Rihanna, 'Work' ended four years of silence from pop's previously most busy star, who famously cranked out seven albums in eight years before taking a break. 'Work' was Rihanna's big comeback, leading directly into *Anti*, her most recent, and as of the time of writing, final album.

For Rihanna especially, dancehall and reggae are baked into her roots in Barbados, while Ariana Grande of course has no such claim to this heritage. Nicki Minaj's guest verse, however, *does* add an air of authenticity to the song, since the MC hails from Trinidad and Tobago. However, I don't think anyone – Grande included – was coming to 'Side To Side' looking to dive into her authenticity. Instead, the song sounds like Max Martin's hitmaking apparatus at work. It's his job to find out what sounds are working in the current moment and extrapolate them. Pop, after all, just means *popular*. When at its best and most honest, pop music is a genre that is a collection of *other* genres, bringing everything into the centre of its own gravity and sending it back out to the masses.

Here, then, the dancehall and reggae aesthetics of 'Work' and 'One Dance' meet crunchy synths and heavy R&B influences running throughout. 'Side To Side' could have very well ended up veering into being filthy, but Grande and Minaj just about manage to toe the line. For the two artists, this was something of a reunion. They had, of course, previously collaborated on 'Bang Bang', but 'Side To Side' was their first time just collaborating with each other (sorry, Jessie J!). Away from the noise of 'Bang Bang', the two artists have extraordinary chemistry on the track and it's no mistake that they would continue to pop up on each other's material after this; they would have a reunion on *Sweetener*'s hypnotic 'The Light Is Coming', while Grande guested vocals to Minaj's 2019 slinky cut, 'Bed'.

Minaj is on fine form here, which is really saying

something because in 2016, she was more than adept at slinging out an eye-catching featured verse to anyone that wanted it. One of her best traits as a lyricist is her humour and 'Side To Side's exaggerated concept gives her more than enough grist to both flex (she confidently states that she is the Queen of Rap and Grande herself runs Pop) and point out the track's inherent strangeness, too. What exactly *is* a dick bicycle? I don't want to know, thanks!

The track's music video is more fashion editorial than visual narrative. Once again helmed by Hannah Lux Davis, it takes the sensible route to use exercise as a visual metaphor for sex. Thus, Grande finds herself in various states of gym classes throughout; she leads a SoulCycle class, she preens to the camera while pretending to box and finally joins up with Minaj in a sauna for her verse. The clip was sponsored by the American clothing brand Guess, which makes sense when you realise that none of these women could conceivably attempt an exercise class in some of their wardrobe choices.

'Side To Side' isn't exactly Grande or Davis' best work together (they would out-do themselves in the *Thank U, Next* era), but the song had results. Bolstered by its music video and a live performance at the 2016 VMAs, where Ariana performed while atop an exercise bike, 'Side To Side' became the second Top 10 single from *Dangerous Woman*, peaking at Number 4 in both the US and the UK. Perhaps even more impressive still, it remains Grande's most-viewed music video on YouTube, with currently over 2.3 billion (!) views.

'Side To Side' was the last big hit of the *Dangerous Woman* era. By the time of its release, Ariana was already planning to tour the globe and as is the way with these things, the release schedule began to power down. One last track would be issued as a single, in January 2017 – the Future collab 'Everyday', which failed to enter the Top 40 in both the US and UK (probably because it wasn't that good – sorry, Ari!).

But perhaps the biggest flex as the era wound down was the Dangerous Woman World Tour. To date, it was Grande's largest and most ambitious live show – a visual representation of her growth and ambition in both her own maturity and her place in the pop pantheon.

Visiting North America, Europe, Asia, Latin America, Australia and New Zealand across six tour legs that stretched across eight months in 2017, the Dangerous Woman Live Show was an event; a wide, expansive stage set, moody lighting to accompany the songs and more intricate choreography than Grande had ever attempted before.

Now twenty-three years old, you can also see this as a very public opportunity for Ariana to signal her growth as a woman. Celebrated stylish Law Roach (best known for his expansive work with the actress Zendaya, turning her into a fashion darling) and designer Bryan Hearns were engaged by Grande to level up her fashion game while on stage. Several facets of her style iconography

– the high ponytail, the platform heels – were still present, but her looks as a whole were designed, Hearns said, to 'making an adult Ariana. Marrying her silhouette with what's happening in fashion right now, so a big theme is sportswear – everything is oversized, there are straps everywhere, and cool hardware . . . It's definitely more edgy, it's more adult, but still playful.'[12]

There's a reason why the show ends with the title track of the album. At that point, it was the most definitive statement Ariana Grande had made on her growth as both an artist and a woman – people only think a strong, confident woman is dangerous because that confidence scares them.

# 5

# The Manchester Bombing and *Sweetener*

The Manchester Arena bombing of 2017 was the deadliest act of terrorism in the UK and the first suicide bombing there since the 7/7 bombings of 2005. The attack took place on 22 May 2017, following the end of Ariana Grande's performance of the Dangerous Woman Tour at the Manchester Arena. The explosive device was detonated at 10.31 p.m. The concert had finished shortly before 10.30 p.m. Attendance at the concert was recorded at 14,200 people.

The explosion instantly killed the bomber, Salman Abedi, along with twenty-two others and injured hundreds more. In an investigation, British intelligence forces listed 1,017 among the injured. The explosion destroyed the foyer of the arena.

Although there have been conflicting reports, Ariana Grande was not on stage during the explosion. She was, at the time, twenty-three years old. To be the face of a tragedy of this magnitude at such a young age seems almost incomprehensible. To her credit, she did not shy away from her responsibilities in the direct aftermath.

Before we get to that, let's pay tribute to the twenty-two victims of the Manchester Arena bombing: Saffie-Rose Roussos. Nell Jones. Sorrell Leczkowski. Eilidh MacLeod. Megan Hurley. Olivia Campbell-Hardy. Chloe Rutherford. Liam Curry. Georgina Callander. Courtney Boyle. John Atkinson. Martyn Hett. Philip Tron. Kelly Brewster. Elaine McIver. Angelika Klis. Marcin Klis. Alison Howe. Lisa Lees. Michelle Kiss. Wendy Fawell. Jane Tweddle. May they rest in peace.

The outpouring of grief following the bombing was swift and all-encompassing. Grande, overcome with grief, swiftly travelled back home to Boca Raton in Florida to be with her family, a choice that no one with a decent moral compass would have any objections to, and cancelled a slate of upcoming tour dates, including a headline show in London. Following the immediate aftermath of the attack, she posted a statement on Twitter saying she was 'broken beyond belief' at what had occurred. For a brief time, it was the most-liked tweet in history. Days later, she would issue a longer statement, sending her 'heart, prayers and deepest condolences' to the victims of the tragedy and their families.

'There is nothing I or anyone can do to take away the pain you are feeling or to make this better,' she wrote. 'However, I extend my hand and heart and everything I possibly can give to you and yours, should you want or need my help in any way.

'The only thing we can do now is choose how we let this affect us and how we live our lives from here on out.'[1]

Many wouldn't have blamed Ariana for retiring away from the spotlight following these events. But she is made of stronger stuff. Within days she had decided to return to Manchester in its darkest hour, a show of strength and empathy that made her into something of a folk hero in the UK. During a visit on 3 June 2017, she called in on the young victims of the attack at the Royal Manchester Children's Hospital. UK media also reported at the time that the singer had offered to cover costs for the victims' funerals, though she never confirmed this publicly.[2]

There was another big reason for her return to Manchester during this time; while away in the US, Grande had decided to do something with her considerable power and influence to pay tribute to the lives lost in the bombing, and also to remind both victims and bystanders of the healing power of music.

Ariana announced that on Sunday, 4 June 2017, she would return to Manchester to play a benefit concert, named One Love Manchester, with all proceeds going towards the victims and their families. She would not be alone; joining her would be an array of some of the biggest A-list pop stars in the world, among them Katy Perry, Justin Bieber and Miley Cyrus, as well as British music legends such as Liam Gallagher, Robbie Williams and Coldplay.

It was a huge undertaking. The idea itself was awe-inspiring, but to see it pulled off in record timing still brings a tear to the eye. One Love Manchester took place at Manchester's Old Trafford Cricket Ground and attracted 55,000 attendees. There was a ballot in place so victims of the tragedy and those present at the Manchester Arena show could claim free tickets to the event. The We Love Manchester Emergency Fund was established by the British Red Cross and Manchester City Council to further help the victims and their families.

One Love Manchester was more than just a concert. Across more than three hours, you saw a city and its people trying to heal and grieve in real time. At first, Ariana was hesitant to play some of her more well-known songs, worrying that playful tracks like 'Break Free' would detract from the tragedy but she was alleviated of this by the mother of fifteen-year-old victim Olivia Campbell-Hardy.

'She told me Olivia wouldn't want to see me cry,' Grande told the crowd on-stage. 'And she would've wanted to hear the hits.'[3]

The structure of the concert itself felt quite loose, in keeping with the quick nature in which it was pulled together, no doubt. There are many, many moments throughout that still bring a tear to the eye to this day; whether it's Robbie Williams' heartfelt rendition of the especially poignant 'Angels', Liam Gallagher's return to his home stomping ground or Ariana serenading the audience with 'My Everything' (a song she rarely sings live to this day) backed by a choir of Manchester school-children, all clearly overcome with emotion.

I think it's the defining act of Grande's career. It was impossible, watching her and her all-star collaborators brought on stage at the end to sing 'One Last Time' together, not to feel incredibly proud of her. Even in the face of adversity, of loss on a colossal scale, Ariana showed the power of love – that's an amazing legacy to leave.

Simulcast on BBC One and across BBC Radio One and Capital FM, One Love Manchester was a global event, livestreamed in over fifty countries. In the UK, it was estimated that the concert averaged 10.9 million viewers on BBC One, with an ultimate peak of 14.5 million. The BBC reported that it was the most-watched television event of 2017, with 22.6 million people watching at least three minutes. Almost half the people in the UK tuned in; the BBC states that One Love Manchester held a 49.6 per cent audience share. The way in which the country embraced the concert and its values is also reflected in the magnificent amounts of money raised.

During the initial three-hour broadcast, the British Red Cross estimated it received £2.35 million in donations. The next day, this figure had risen to £10 million. *Billboard* later reported that the all-time donations tally stood at £17 million and that each of the families of the twenty-two victims of the attack would receive £243,000.

The link between Ariana Grande and Manchester is now inextricable and forever. Following the concert, the singer was made an honorary citizen of Manchester and it was reported that she had 'politely declined' an honorary damehood to mark her charitable work for the victims of the bombing.[4] There was some controversy when, in 2019, dates for the Sweetener Tour didn't include a stop in Manchester, but this was simply because she had already made secret plans to headline that year's Manchester Pride, the first time she had performed in the city since One Love Manchester.

One question remained, though: how would she move on from this trauma, and how would it be reflected in her music?

The answer to that was *Sweetener* (2018), by far her most experimental album. She could have made a record of contemplative, maudlin ballads, but *Sweetener* is, instead, an alternative pop album that is much more interested in discovering how one can move on from grief. At its core, it's a sentimentally positive work, characterised by the many risks Grande and her collaborators would take in the production of its songs.

The regular suspects of both Tommy Brown, Max Martin and Ilya all return from *Dangerous Woman*, but perhaps the biggest headline from the making of the album was that Ariana had written tracks with Pharrell.

Pharrell Williams came to fame as one half of the production duo The Neptunes, who cranked out a series of early '00s hits for the likes of Britney Spears ('I'm A Slave 4 U'), Justin Timberlake ('Rock Your Body') and Kelis ('Milkshake'). He is an enduring figure in pop culture, noted for his boundary-pushing hits and eye-catching fashion sense.

Although, by 2018, Pharrell's hitmaking, boundary-pushing peak was behind him following his hits at the start of the decade with Robin Thicke's 'Blurred Lines' with T.I. and his own 'Happy', the statement of working with him was an effective signpost of Ariana's growing star-power. Though it's also an interesting fact to note that none of the songs she worked on with Pharrell were released as official singles during *Sweetener*'s promo run.

Still, the work she and Pharrell did on this album is impressive in just how strange and against the grain for her it was. *Sweetener* is the sound of Grande finding out what works for her in this new stage of her life. She was going through personal changes that would affect her deeply in the next few years too; her two-year relationship with Mac Miller would come to an end in May 2018. Just two weeks after their breakup, Miller was arrested for a DUI offence, with US tabloid *Page Six* reporting that his blood-alcohol level was more than two times over the legal limit.[5]

As usual, the internet was the dumping ground for some of humanity's most toxic opinions. Grande notably replied to one Miller fan, essentially blaming her for Miller's legal troubles due to the breakup.

'I am not a babysitter or a mother and no woman should feel that they need to be,' she replied in a now-deleted tweet. 'I have cared from him and tried to support his sobriety & prayed for his balance for years (and always will of course) but shaming/blaming women for a man's inability to keep his shit together is a very major problem.'[6]

Soon after she would embark on a whirlwind romance with comedian Pete Davidson, the two having met backstage at *Saturday Night Live*, where Davidson was a cast member. Just weeks after meeting, the pair would announce their engagement. Davidson joked that it 'felt like [he'd] won a contest'.[7]

The fast pace of the relationship, and how outwardly the two promoted it on their social media at the time, made both Grande and Davidson tabloid fodder.

While *Thank U, Next* deals explicitly with the eventual fallout of her failed engagement to Davidson, *Sweetener* does have one track that directly references the new relationship. 'Pete Davidson' (subtle) preserves the honeymoon phase for posterity's sake, as the album's last-but-one song.

*Sweetener* is held in high regard by both critics and fans alike, many of whom state this is Grande's best work. I would disagree, but I think it's a stepping stone to her *actual* magnum opus, *Thank U, Next*, and the two records are so heavily in conversation with one another, it can be hard to separate them.

But it's amazing just how much Ariana stretches herself on this record. *Sweetener* returned her to the top of the Billboard album charts, debuting at Number 1 with 231,000 copies – a record for her at that time as her highest first-week sales. Added into this total were

126.7 million on-demand streams, which at the time set a record for the highest first-week streams for a non-hip hop album by a female artist. The year 2018 was the apex of the streaming boom, a democratisation of listening habits that had, up until this point, largely benefited rap acts like Drake or Future, whose release schedules were much more fluid and frequent than the tried-and-tested cycle of 'single, album, tour' that had defined pop music for much of the twenty-first century.

At the time, *Billboard* reported that *Sweetener*'s streaming dominance was rare for a wholesale pop act[8] but what no one could predict was that for Grande's next trick, she would move away from a stereotypical pop-star release campaign and change the game while making the defining music of her career.

GEORGE GRIFFITHS

## 'ONE LAST TIME'

**Release date:** 10 February 2015
**Written by:** Savan Kotecha, David Guetta, Carl Falk, Rami, Giorgio Tuinfort
**Produced by:** Carl Falk, Rami

'One Last Time' may have been released more than two years before the Manchester Arena bombing, but it came to define the days, weeks and months after the attack. In the shadow of this tragedy, of all the grief, anger and fear, this delicate plea for one last night with the person you love, to live in the moment even though you know it will not last, that it *cannot* last, found its true potential as an anthem.

'One Last Time' had originally been released as the final single from *My Everything*, while Ariana was touring the record in 2015. As we've discussed, *My Everything* was a big step up for our girl; it allowed her to unlock a previously hidden level of pop stardom that she hadn't been able to reach on *Yours Truly*. One of my favourite things about it is that it really sounds nothing like the other songs pegged as singles from that record. 'Problem' and 'Break Free' were in-your-face in the best way, while the restraint present in 'Love Me Harder' didn't take away from the fact that it was a meeting of the minds with The Weeknd.

'One Last Time' has no such pleasure in peacocking, or headline-grabbing collaborations, though superstar

DJ David Guetta is credited as both a writer and a producer on the track. 'One Last Time' is one of Grande's most sincere singles. Its high-concept music video is shot in a first-person POV as Ariana and her *Victorious* co-star Matt Bennett are cast as a couple who experience a world-ending apocalypse and it was helmed by Max Landis, who famously wrote the script for acclaimed 2011 superhero film, *Chronicle*.

The pleasure of 'One Last Time' lies in its tender production, which at various points recalls electronica, and the work of artists such as Robyn and a *Ray Of Light*-era Madonna. Grande's voice on the track is the perfect clash between yearning and total honesty. During its chorus, you can hear whispered snippets in the background, giving you the feeling that you've just overheard her giving into her barely contained desires. It's a lot more of a mature offering than initially given credit for and is a clear foundation for the excellent work she would replicate nearly a decade later on *Eternal Sunshine*.

But the loss of the thrill of maximalism was felt upon the song's initial release as a single. During its first runaround, 'One Last Time' became the first of Grande's *My Everything* singles to miss the US Top 10, thus ending a four-song long streak, peaking at Number 13. It fared worse in the UK, missing the Top 20 entirely and reaching Number 24. It didn't help, of course, that the *My Everything* era was coming to an end and it's usually the case that the last single from an album campaign has a more muted reception, mostly because more often than not, new material is already being worked on.

It was during the face of unimaginable trauma and violence, though, that 'One Last Time' would finally get its dues. In the immediate aftermath of the Manchester Arena attack, the song became the anointed anthem of the time, a paean to the lives lost and the time with them left unspent.

A passionate fan campaign in the days leading on from the bombing saw the song begin to rise in real time as people reckoned with the real-world trauma that had just unfolded. In a nod to the campaign, Ariana performed 'One Last Time' at One Love Manchester, the last-but-one song of the night. She took to the stage alongside every single act that had participated in the concert, leading a sing-along with the crowd, Ariana herself clearly overcome with emotion.

Now re-released as a single, 'One Last Time' shot up to Number 2 in the UK's Official Singles Chart, denied its rightful chart-topper status for two consecutive weeks by Luis Fonsi, Daddy Yankee and Justin Bieber's 'Despacito' remix.

It is now, of course, impossible to separate this song from the tragedy that came to define its success, but I find this only imbues it with *more* emotion. Now, 'One Last Time' is not just a pop song, it's a hymn to those we have lost, and all the time, still unspent, that went with them.

ARIANA GRANDE

## 'NO TEARS LEFT TO CRY'

**Release date:** 20 April 2018
**Written by:** Ariana Grande, Max Martin, Ilya, Savan Kotecha
**Produced by:** Max Martin, Ilya

Healing is hard. Trying to bounce back from a trauma that was broadcast on the global stage? That's nigh on impossible. But this was the task facing Ariana Grande as she approached the release of her fourth album.

But healing doesn't happen in a straight line. With 'No Tears Left to Cry', the lead single of *Sweetener*, Grande drops you right in the middle of her process of letting the light in. As I mentioned earlier, no one would have blamed the singer for starting this era with a timely ballad directly referencing the Manchester attack and its effect on both her and the victims' families. Yet, it was a stroke of genius that *Sweetener*'s first single *is* a response to all that Grande has endured – just not in the way you might think. 'No Tears Left to Cry' doesn't sound like a pleading hymn for love and understanding in dark times. Instead, it's a hopeful and buoyant ode to choosing to live. To acknowledge that darkness exists, and can affect us, but you must never let it consume you.

Despite her extensive work with Pharrell for the skeleton of *Sweetener*, it does make sense that for the album's starting gun, Ariana would turn to Max Martin and co. Pharrell's work, for all its funk and experimental verve, tends to shy away from anything that isn't a solidly positive emotion. But pop music has to do more than embrace positivity, it must deal with the contrasting sides of human nature and experience too. 'No Tears Left to Cry' was, by Grande's own admission, a statement of intent to not be defined by negativity. The song's co-writer, Savan Kotecha, told *Billboard* in an interview around the time of the release that its title came about during a writing session with Grande when she spoke about her intentions for the song.

'I want it to be positive,' Kotecha recalled her saying. '[I want to] talk about positivity and love. I don't have any tears left to cry.'[9]

The track's intentions were obvious from the off. When Grande posted the single cover artwork, it was clear we weren't going to dwell on the past. In one of her most striking portraits, the return of Ariana Grande has seen our favourite pop star shift and change. She's photographed facing to the right, her hair now dyed a purple so light, it's almost translucent. Gone, too, is her signature high ponytail, now set low down to the nape of her neck. She looks in front of her, away from the camera, as the colours of the rainbow shine on her face. It was a very real signal that she would be stepping away from the darkness now and into the light. She was about to turn twenty-five years old and this was a very real moment of growth. She was a woman changed, but resilient.

As such, the song drops us right in the middle of

Ariana's healing process. Just like the title tells us, her time crying – and therefore grieving – is over. Now, it's time to try and move on. To live and love in the sunlight. In keeping with the experimental nature of *Sweetener*, 'No Tears Left to Cry' seems to chug along, defying your expectations of what it *should* sound like and having a very good time doing so too.

It tricks you right from the off. The opening bars are stark and almost gospel in nature, with just Grande's voice – and the sentiment that she is so upset, she doesn't want to leave her house – booming. One would think this would be the emotional throughline to the song, dramatic and leering into Barbra Streisand-esque balladry, but almost immediately, Max Martin and Ilya's production picks up, and the rest of the track blooms. The song never directly addresses the events that unfolded in Manchester a year prior, although the heavy garage influences during its verses can't help but be read as a none-too-subtle nod to the UK.

'No Tears Left to Cry' didn't sound like any other pop track released in 2018 – and indeed, it made several best-of-year lists from outlets like the *Guardian* and *Stereogum* – and its bracing approach to real-world events gave it a startling injection of authenticity. More than that, though, this was a foundational moment for Ariana Grande as an artist. We've spoken about how previous releases had flirted with their artist's real-life experiences, but 'No Tears Left to Cry' is the first time we can see her directly pulling from her own life story and weaving that story into the narrative of her music. The effects were startling (it's no mistake that less than six months later, her next album would be made almost in tandem with the events of her life at that point).

More striking still is the track's music video, the first (but not the last) of Grande's visuals to be helmed by visionary director Dave Meyers, who has shot all-time classics like Missy Elliott's 'Work It', Aaliyah's 'More Than A Woman' and Kendrick Lamar's 'Humble'. He brings a similarly deft touch to this shoot; the world of 'No Tears Left to Cry' is one of a cityscape turned upside down and in on itself. Visually, it recalls the heady dream sequences from Christopher Nolan's *Inception*. In the video, Grande – her hair dyed a starlight grey, eschewing her high ponytail for a braid and low-slung ponytail, pointing to her evolution and elevation in the time between releases – tries to find her way out of the chaos and back to acceptance. I've always thought that the opening sequence of the video, with a gospel choir, should have been the introduction to the actual song, giving it a grandiose and operatic feel totally in touch with the various emotions she is working through during its run-time. The clip ends with Grande, finding peace at last, looking over the water as a bee – the symbol for the city of Manchester – flies past the camera.

'This was the centrepiece for the *Sweetener* album and era,' Ariana told *Allure*. '[The video for 'No Tears Left to Cry'] is a play on being so upside down, you don't know what's right or what is up. Personally, in my life at the time, I *was* upside down and not knowing where the ground was. I didn't feel very safe or OK. It was a really cool way to visually represent how I was feeling.'[10]

The world was ready to embrace 'No Tears Left to Cry' and embrace it they did, completely. In May 2018, the track debuted at Number 3 in the US and were it not for Drake holding the top-two spots with 'Nice For What' (his best-ever song) and 'God's Plan', Ariana would have secured her first US chart-topper. Overall, the track spent twelve non-consecutive weeks in the US Top 10. In the UK, in May 2018, 'No Tears Left to Cry' peaked at Number 2, held off for two weeks by summer smash 'One Kiss' by Calvin Harris and Dua Lipa.

Returning to pop music after everything Ariana had endured in 2017 was an insurmountable task. I can't think of many artists who wouldn't have buckled under that pressure. But on 'No Tears Left to Cry', she gave us a defiant statement and proved that during the time she'd taken away from music, she had unlocked a previously hidden level of her artistry.

GEORGE GRIFFITHS

## 'GOD IS A WOMAN'

**Release date:** 13 July 2018
**Written by:** Ariana Grande, Ilya, Max Martin, Savan Kotecha, Rickard Göransson
**Produced by:** Ilya

On 'God Is A Woman', Ariana Grande wants you to confess and genuflect. A standout track on *Sweetener*, it is clear that the inclusion is more down to its obvious potential as a hit rather than its adherence to the record's integral themes.

In fact, we *know* the song started its life without Grande. It was written by Max Martin, Ilya, Savan Kotecha and Wolf Cousins member Rickard Göransson and originally pitched to Camila Cabello, who by 2018 had split from Fifth Harmony and was hard at work on her debut solo album *Camila*. The original demo for Cabello was leaked as a duet with British-Kosovian pop star Rita Ora, who was experiencing something of a second wind in her hitmaking career at the time. But the collaboration was seemingly scrapped, the one surviving demo on the internet being markedly different to the version Grande released.

Grande indeed made sizeable changes to her take on the song, more than earning that co-writer credit! In her hands, 'God Is A Woman' transforms, taking the subtle hip-hop influences present in 'No Tears Left to Cry' and enlarging them. Here, she now spends the verses rapping over trap-influenced beats, her flow and inflections mirroring Drake and Nicki Minaj. It's one of the first times we can hear her *yuh!*, now a hallmark of her cadence.

'God Is A Woman' is a return to the unapologetic pop star domination of the *Yours Truly* and *Dangerous Woman* eras. It's unashamedly flashy and another instance where Ariana is now more comfortable talking about sex. In fact, she's so confident that one night spent with her and you'll genuinely start to worship her as if she's a deity. One of the most gorgeous choices Martin and Ilya make on the production is to layer her voice over and over, so by the end, when the hook is repeated one last time, she is backed by a choir of her own voice. It sounds like she's steadily collected acolytes who are now ready to kneel down to her at an altar.

Worship is also on the agenda for the track's music video, the kind of balls-to-the-walls, everything-and-the-kitchen-sink type pop visual that we had sadly been lacking since Lady Gaga's heyday in the early 2010s, when cuts like 'Bad Romance', 'Alejandro' and 'Judas' were fit to bursting with religious and socio-political subtext, alongside the typical opulent backdrops and choreography-heavy routines we've come to expect as par for the course for pop's upper echelon of stars.

Once again directed by Dave Meyers, the video for 'God Is A Woman' is absolutely ridiculous in the best possible way. Not only featuring Grande swimming in a vulva-shaped pool or, in the most memorable set-piece, straddling the world and penetrating it with her fingers, she and Meyers make quick work of several references to antiquity, such as the Roman Pantheon, *The Creation of Adam* and the image of the Capitoline Wolf. Combining this with more recent references to the work of Kendrick Lamar and Madonna's conical bra, 'God Is A Woman' is an exercise in trying to bridge the gap between the ancient and the modern, the divine and the mortal. But perhaps the best reference of all is saved for the moment in the video where the music drops out and we hear a very familiar female voice begin to recite Ezekiel 25:15, a nod to Samuel L. Jackson's own monologue in Quentin Tarantino's 1994 masterpiece, *Pulp Fiction*. Who is that voice, I hear you ask? Oh, only the Queen of Pop herself – Madonna!

This is Ariana giving thanks and (literal) praise to someone who led the way for the female artists who followed in her wake and a nod to the 'Like A Prayer' inspiration of the song. Talking to US late-night host Jimmy Fallon, Ariana said that she asked Madonna to take part in the video shoot by 'texting' her and that her inclusion was a celebration of everything she had achieved and fought for.

'[Madonna] paved the way for all of us,' Ariana said. 'She has been fighting that fight way longer than any of us. Without her, I wouldn't have been able to make [a song titled 'God Is A Woman'].'[11]

Following this, Ariana seemed more interested in broadcasting 'God Is A Woman' as a feminist anthem, rather than just a song about sex. During her performance of the track at the 2018 MTV VMA Awards (which might just take the title of my favourite Grande live performance ever, actually), she recreates da Vinci's *The Last Supper* in real time with an all-female cast and ends the performance with welcoming her mother, Joan Grande, her beloved Nonna, Marjorie Grande, and her cousin, Lani Crane, on stage. Together, they join hands with her in perfect harmony.

Given the media blitz around Grande at this time, especially since she had attended the VMAs with Pete Davidson after announcing their engagement following a whirlwind romance, all eyes were on her for this moment. Tabloid buzz or no, 'God Is A Woman' was one of the most impressive performances of the night and affected the song's chart performance in a very real way.

Initially, 'God Is A Woman' debuted at Number 11 on the Billboard Hot 100 but by the time of the August VMAs, the song had sufficient strength to shoot into the Top 10 for the first time and reached its peak of Number 8, becoming Grande's landmark tenth Top 10 single at the same time. Over in the UK, 'God Is A Woman' debuted and peaked at Number 4.

## 'BREATHIN'

**Release date:** 18 September 2018
**Written by:** Ariana Grande, Savan Kotecha, Ilya, Peter Svensson
**Produced by:** Ilya

'I've always had anxiety,' Ariana Grande once told British *Vogue*. 'But I never [spoke about it publicly] because I thought everyone had it.'[12]

At its height, anxiety can be overwhelming to the ninth degree, but even when that dissipates, its taste lingers in the air. You end up anticipating its next arrival, preparing for it even.

More so than any track on *Sweetener*, 'Breathin' deals in more certain terms with Ariana's own personal fallout from the Manchester Arena bombing. Following the attack, she was formally diagnosed with post-traumatic stress disorder (PTSD) and had to learn to use breathing exercises to combat her growing anxiety, especially in public places or in crowds.

For Ariana, her experience of anxiety was a very physical thing. Her symptoms would manifest in the most disorientating way possible, giving her vertigo and dizzy spells. These symptoms got steadily worse after she returned home from the Dangerous Woman World Tour (following the Manchester attacks, seven shows were cancelled and she finished the tour in September 2017 after legs in Australia, New Zealand and Asia) and for a brief time paused work on the album that would become *Sweetener*.

'Breathin' is one of the strongest songs on *Sweetener*. It functions as something of a perfect sequel to 'No Tears Left to Cry'. While 'No Tears Left to Cry' finds its strength in Grande willing her listeners to follow her into the light and to dry their tears, 'Breathin' is more introspective and altogether knottier.

There is something of an age-old adage that pop stars cannot be fallible; that they must be placed on a pedestal high above us and shine like the gods on Olympus. In this sense, they cannot be allowed to show any faults because this would betray the illusion and expose them as not gods, but human after all.

At least, that was the train of thought until recently. One of the most fascinating things about watching pop music and its central muses evolve over the last decade has been seeing the real time turn away from a star's perceived invulnerability as a strength, to the general public's need to now see their favourite musicians as authentic – and incredibly human.

This applies more to acts such as Billie Eilish, SZA and Charli xcx than it does Grande, but 'Breathin' is another marker of Ariana's growing fascination with introspection in her music and how this almost perfectly aligns with a change in the public's listening trends. The year 2018, when she released *Sweetener*, was smack bang in the middle of two debut albums that defined this new era of pop: SZA's 2017 LP *Ctrl* and Billie Eilish's *When*

*We All Fall Asleep, Where Do We Go?* in 2019. The impact of these two records on pop music was meteoric and marked the shift into an era where streaming became the dominant form of music consumption.

Ariana has said that her pivot to exploring more personal topics in her music was born out of a sense of 'urgency' during a very turbulent time in her life. Speaking on *The Hollywood Reporter*'s podcast, she posits it that '[during that time] I was doing so much therapy, and I was dealing with PTSD and all different kinds of grief and depression and anxiety.'

She credits her music as 'the remedy that absolutely saved my life' and describes how 'it poured out with urgency, and it was made with urgency'.[13]

You can see the beginnings of this more diaristic lyricism in 'Breathin', like the anxiety that she is feeling can only be counteracted by her honesty about the state of her mental health and how she has learnt to cope with it. It's gorgeously backed by Ilya's production, shimmering with synths and the biggest strength, a cacophony of 808 drums that get more and more intense as the song continues, exploding into the final chorus, every emotion that Grande is feeling laid bare before us. She *has* to keep breathing, she tells us. There is no other way. She can't be defined or dragged by this moment. There is no choice but to go on and to hope that one day it will get better. The drums carry us forward, literally instructing us to march on, forward.

The complex feelings are perfectly articulated and

given life by director Hannah Lux Davis in the track's music video. We see Grande's PTSD manifest in the middle of a train station. Her vision becomes blurred and the people around her all seem to mould together. The world is moving too fast for her and she needs to slow down. To do this, Davis filmed Grande with motion control photography, meaning that she would be filmed at a slower frame rate than the extras around her, giving the illusion she is out of step with the world around her.

This is intercepted with some of the most stunning glamour shots in all of Grande's videography, Davis casting her in a room filled with smoke that continues to obstruct her from the camera or standing alone with a thundering cloud covering her eyes or, in the video's emotional closing moments, sat on a swing, high above the atmosphere, surrounded by nothing but blue sky and clouds. A vision of an anxiety-free existence that, for those suffering with the condition, can at times feel like nothing but a dream.

'Breathin' was a fan favourite track from the moment of *Sweetener*'s release, so its status as a future single was never in doubt. But tragic circumstances beyond anyone's control would mean that its time in the sun would be cut short. The official release, on 18 September 2018, came just a few weeks after Ariana's ex-boyfriend, the rapper Mac Miller, died of a drug overdose on 7 September 2018. Miller was just twenty-six years old. His passing would affect not only Ariana's personal life but her music too. Instead of stepping away from music and healing in private, as had been in the case in 2017, she would take this moment to work through her complicated feelings on grief and loss in almost real time. She would gather her closest collaborators and friends around her to make the most singular record in her discography, and one of the best pop records in recent memory.

# 6

## *Thank U, Next* and the Magic of the Imperial Phase

The notion of an 'imperial phase', the section of a pop star's career where they reach the zenith of their commercial and critical success, was originally coined by Neil Tennant of the Pet Shop Boys. As Tennant defines it,[1] an imperial phase is when a pop star enters an era in which they can do no wrong. Everything that their career up to this point had been a fight for – whether commercial recognition or being taken seriously by media outlets that may have ignored them in the past – seems to be achieved with ease. In an imperial phase, an act can be relied on making the best music of their career, enamouring fans and critics alike (for what it's worth, Tennant reckons the Pet Shop Boys' own imperial phase straddled 1988–89, a period in which they released their most successful album, *Actually*, and three of the band's four UK Number 1 singles, including their best-known hits, 'It's A Sin' and 'Always On My Mind').

Towards the close of 2018, Ariana Grande is

twenty-five years old. She has already seen meteoric success, but also battled severe depression and trauma. It's more than some artists ever get to fit into an entire career. But Ariana was only just getting started. She was about to begin the *Thank U, Next* era and, as a direct consequence of this, her imperial phase.

There is no question about that. For a period of around ten months – from November 2018 to September 2019 with the release of 'Thank U, Next', the single up until the launch of 'Don't Call Me Angel' – Ariana Grande was the best and most interesting pop star in the world. Not only did she release her magnum opus, she finally clinched that long sought-after US Number 1 single *and* began to receive the kind of plaudits and adoration so rarely afforded to a commercial pop act.

To understand why, suddenly, everything was going right for Grande around this time, we need to understand why *Thank U, Next* stands so monolithic not just in her own discography, but in the wider context of pop music in the 2010s.

*Thank U, Next* is not only a stunning artistic accomplishment – a record of incredible anger and empathy, of emancipation and pain, grief and euphoria mixed together in a potent cocktail with tears and champagne – but particularly impressive, given a record this self-analytical was produced during a time in which Grande's celebrity was at an all-time high.

Part of the impact this era had was on Grande's own star persona and the overwhelming media attention on her at this time, so much so that much of the album's creation and release was almost captured minute-for-minute through paparazzi lenses and people's Twitter timelines. It's a connection between the personal and the public, between healing and self-destruction. *Thank U, Next*, as a body of work, interrogates the nebulous undergrowth between all these things. It digs deep into the earth and comes back bearing diamonds, mined from Ariana's own body and soul. It must have been an incredibly painful process to go through, mentally and physically not just creatively, but no one can argue with the results. To say that they are stunning is an understatement.

*Thank U, Next* was conceived in a maelstrom. The first foundational act of its creation was one of tragedy: the death of Ariana's ex-boyfriend, Mac Miller, on 18 September 2018. Miller had been open and honest about his struggles with substance abuse in his music. He was found unresponsive at his Los Angeles home by his personal assistant and pronounced dead at the scene. He was just twenty-six years old. In the months following his death, a coroner's report confirmed his death was the result of an accidental drug overdose. Fentanyl, cocaine and alcohol were found in his system.

Upon the announcement of Miller's death, Ariana paid tribute to her 'dearest friend', saying that he was the 'kindest, sweetest soul with demons he never deserved'.[2] The relationship between the pair had broken down that May and in a statement at the time, Ariana more or less confirmed that Miller's struggles with addiction had contributed to the breakup.[3]

She described her grief over his death in 2018 as 'all-consuming' but was also very candid with *Vogue* about how, like many people whose partners have addiction issues, their relationship couldn't be sustained under such a strain.

'We weren't perfect,' she said. 'But, like, fuck. He was the best person. He didn't deserve the demons he had. I was the glue for such a long time and I felt myself becoming less and less sticky. The pieces just started to float away.'[4]

In the immediate aftermath, promotion of *Sweetener* and its newest single, 'Breathin', were swiftly cancelled by Republic Records, although Ariana soon returned to the studio, beginning recording for the album that would become *Thank U, Next* by October.

Talking to the *Hollywood Reporter* in 2024, she admitted that her label was 'hesitant' to move into a brand new album era so soon as 'it wasn't really something that [pop stars] did'.

'I said, "I don't care about that,"' she recalled. 'I didn't want to play by any rules. It's what I needed for my soul.'[5]

There was no doubt that the after-effects of Miller's death had ripples, both on the recording session and Ariana's own personal life. At the time, she was engaged to comedian Pete Davidson following a whirlwind romance that had been captured from the start and analysed endlessly by the media (and fans on social media).

She recalled to *Vogue* how she and Davidson had reconnected after friends convinced her to summer in New York following her split with Miller prior to his death.

'I met Pete and it was an amazing distraction,' she said candidly. 'It was frivolous and fun and insane and highly unrealistic, and I loved him, and I didn't know him.'[6]

Work on the record was only compounded when Ariana's engagement to Davidson came to an end, almost as quickly as their relationship had flourished (media reports stated that the pair started casually dating just two weeks after her breakup with Miller). Two weeks into October, multiple outlets reported that they had decided to part ways after a particularly tumultuous time, given the recurring trauma over Miller's death.[7]

Davidson himself has opened up in the past about just how fractious Miller's death was in his relationship with Grande, admitting he 'pretty much knew it was over' in the days following news breaking of the rapper's passing.

'That [entire situation] was really horrible,' he told radio host Charlamagne Tha God. 'I can't imagine what that shit is like. All I do know is that she really loved the shit out [of Miller]. She wasn't putting on a show or anything.'[8]

These two events go hand in hand throughout all of *Thank U, Next*, which was conceptualised and recorded in almost record time. Given her personal struggles during this time, Ariana worked incredibly quickly and made sure to surround herself with a crack team of the closest collaborators throughout her career. At first this was Tommy Brown and Victoria Monét, along with the production duo Social House (Michael Foster and Charles Anderson) and songwriter Tayla Parx, who helped her whip through nine tracks in just a fortnight. Apparently, for these sessions, Ariana made sure that champagne was available on tap.

Grande's work with Brown and Monét always carried the emotional bandwidth of her previous albums and it's here in *Thank U, Next* that their work is truly allowed to fill up the space it deserves. The trio do their best work here, helping to ensure that Grande and Monét's lyrics – trite, sharp and honest to a point – are fulfilled by luxuriant and at times spiky productions that blur the line between Top 40 pop, modern-day R&B and bouncy trap beats. The one-two punch of the title track and '7 rings' are obvious pointers enough to Grande moving in to make the best music of her career, but there's also the buoyant 'NASA', an ode to needing more space and the confessional 'Needy', which sounds like a more modern take on a classic Mariah Carey record and shows just how much Ariana has grown artistically since her debut as this doesn't feel like an impersonation anymore, but her own specific take on the genre.

Brought in to help finish things, of course, was everyone's favourite crack team of Swedish pop wizards:

Who's that girl! Aged just 15 (!), Ariana Grande made her professional debut as a cast member of the Broadway musical *13*, which ran from 2008–2009. During its run, Ariana would meet long-time friend and future *Victorious* co-star Liz Gillies, as well as collaborate for the first time with producer and composer Jason Robert Brown.

*Left* Ariana's big breakthrough came with the role of the hapless Cat Valentine on the Nickelodeon musical-comedy *Victorious*, set in a performing arts high school in LA. *Victorious* ran for four seasons, while Ariana would go on to reprise the role of Cat for a single-season spin-off, *Sam & Cat*.

*Below* The release of Ariana's debut album, *Yours Truly*, was a watermark moment for her career, helping to establish her as one of the most popular and fastest-rising pop stars of her era. Here, she's pictured celebrating its release at an event held in a Best Buy in California. You've got to start somewhere, girl!

Ariana's relationship with the rapper Mac Miller (l) was one of the most impactful throughout the first decade of her career. The two collaborated on her first hit single, 'The Way', before striking up a relationship from 2016–2018. Miller's death from a drug overdose in September 2018 would serve as a catalyst for both the breakdown of Ariana's engagement to comedian Pete Davidson, and the genesis for her magnum opus, *Thank U, Next*.

An emotional end to Ariana's landmark One Love Manchester tribute concert for the victims of the Manchester Arena bombing. Ariana memorably closed out the show by performing a cover of Judy Garland's 'Over The Rainbow', and she also gave a rendition of 'One Last Time', backed by an all-star choir including the likes of Katy Perry, Miley Cyrus, Little Mix and her all-time idol, Imogen Heap.

During a performance of 'God Is A Woman' at the 2018 VMAs, Grande was joined live on stage by (l-r) her cousin Lani Crane, beloved grandmother Marjorie 'Nonna' Grande and her mother, Joan Grande.

Do you hear the thunder coming down? Ariana joins Lady Gaga on stage at the MTV VMAs in 2020 for the live debut of 'Rain On Me'. This is the first, and so far only, time the two artists have performed their chart-topping disco track together.

*Above* Ariana arrives at the New York premiere of *Wicked* with co-star Cynthia Erivo. The film – the first of a duology – would prove to be a huge commercial and critical success, as well as netting both actresses Oscar nominations for their respective roles as Galinda and Elphaba.

*Right* A rare treat indeed, one of the most public instances of Ariana interacting with her current partner, *Wicked* co-star Ethan Slater. The two met while filming in London, and have kept their relationship notoriously private.

During the 2025 Academy Awards, Ariana helped open the ceremony, performing both a cover of 'Over The Rainbow' and 'Defying Gravity' with Cynthia Erivo. Ariana was nominated for Best Supporting Actress at the ceremony but would lose the Oscar to Zoe Saldaña.

*Above* Anyone fancy a trip to the Emerald City? Ariana and Cynthia Erivo attend the London premiere of *Wicked*. Ariana's eye-catching yellow dress and green spectacles were a direct reference to the musical's original Broadway run, when Kristin Chenoweth (who originated the role of Galinda) wore a similar outfit onstage during her arrival to Emerald City.

*Left* Besties! One of the best things about *Wicked* was its iconic (and a little chaotic) press tour, when Ariana and Cynthia Erivo's eccentricities were on full show – and we are still holding space for them. Bring on the press tour for the sequel, girls!

Max Martin, Ilya and Savan Kotecha, who contributed the slickest, more pop-leaning bangers. Part of *Thank U, Next*'s brilliance is that these all feel *so* cohesive and in conversation with each other, rather than the work of separate teams; Grande, her experiences and her voice are the golden thread tying everything together. There is the saxxy 'Bloodline' or my personal pick as the record's best track, 'Bad idea', where she leans extravagantly into trap-pop and gives us a semi-sequel to 'Into You'. 'Bad idea' is about giving into your worst instincts, when you *know* it's wrong, and Grande's peculiar way of enunciating the title (*bahhhd eye-dee-yuh!*) or the way that the song decides to dissect itself in its closing moments, a hint that these actions do indeed have consequences.

But perhaps the most affecting song on *Thank U, Next* – a track that seems to personify its shattered yet still-beating heart – would require the work of these two disparate teams to bring it together whole. 'Ghostin' is the most affecting and effective song on *Thank U, Next*; able to communicate Grande's intense trauma and guilt over the passing of Mac Miller and her eventual, inevitable breakup with Davidson through some truly heaven-sent melodies. It was the hardest song to get right; being the first one she worked on during recording and the last one finished, combining both Monét's talents and the work of Martin, Kotecha and Ilya to bring it to a finish. Grande has, to this day, never performed it live.

*Thank U, Next* was written quickly, finished quickly and released quickly too. The promotional campaign for the record more or less eschewed the standard rollout we've come to expect for a pop star of Ariana's calibre. This, it turned out, was intentional and would have wide-ranging consequences for her peers and successors as a result.

*Thank U, Next*'s first single, its title track, was issued on 3 November 2018 with the full album following a little over three months later, on 8 February 2019. There was a fluidity to its release that, to Ariana's own admission, emulated the release schedule of a rapper. Artists like Drake and Future have always been more adept at recording material and dropping it soon after inception, whereas most pop campaigns contain songs written several months if not years earlier.

'Unless it was rap or hip-hop,' Ariana commented on quick-release schedules, 'it wasn't really a commonly done thing.'[9]

This ability to transcend the gears of the pop music machine – something Grande had very much been made to work in tandem with and in service of earlier in her career – marked a career-changing moment for her. This was now no ordinary pop star.

It's interesting, then, that *Thank U, Next* is a work concerned with breaking free from the chains that constrain you, whether from grief, a relationship you know has reached its natural end or even just the doubting voices in your own head. Even on its now-iconic cover, Grande pulls a similar trick to the cover of *Sweetener* (forever connecting the two LPs as sister records), where she's photographed upside down. Whereas on *Sweetener*'s cover, she seems composed and dare I say it hopeful, staring off into the distance, on *Thank U, Next*, she seems in a state of disarray. Her chest is bare, the title of the album written on it in thick black marker, almost like a spider's web. Her eyes are closed and her face turned away from the camera, while her hair is tangled and hanging loose in a ponytail as if caught in a tornado. It seems to convey a sense of chaos and of messiness, that the healing she had preached about so earnestly on *Sweetener* is, for the moment, delayed. Now is her time to exist in the centre of the hurricane, to try and bypass the chaos in her life.

When the full record was released in February, Ariana was coming off the back of a double Number 1 single streak in her native US and had the largest stage possible through which the world could receive this new album. You know what they say, Number 1 singles are like buses – you spend so long waiting for one, then two come along at the same time.

*Thank U, Next* was a sensation with both fans and critics alike. It's the kind of album that resonated so far and so deep that even people who didn't know who Ariana Grande was a year before now not only knew who she was, but listened to (and loved) the music she was making.

Given the media firestorm around her at the time, the album of course pulled in enviable numbers during its first week on sale. *Thank U, Next* debuted at Number 1 in the US with 360,000 units. Not only Grande's highest-ever first week sales, but the biggest opening week for a female pop act since commercial juggernaut Taylor Swift's *reputation* two years previously. It also marked her second US Number 1 album in less than six months, the quickest accumulation of chart-topping LPs since Olivia Newton-John (!) in the 1970s. *Thank U, Next*'s streaming numbers were a big part in its success; there were 307 million on-demand streams during its first week, a record at the time for both a female artist and a pop album.

Despite being released right at the start of the year, *Thank U, Next* ended 2019 as many publication's picks for one of the best albums of the year, including *Rolling Stone*, and it was later named the eighth-best album of the 2010s by *Billboard*, just eight months after it first entered the world.

At the 2020 Grammy Awards, the most important night in American music, Ariana Grande was one of the evening's most distinguished nominees, pulling in five nominations, including the two biggest awards of the night, Album of the Year for *Thank U, Next* and Record of the Year for the album's title track. She wouldn't win any of these nominations, but *Thank U, Next* had made such an impact that when accepting her Album of the Year Grammy for *When We All Fall Asleep, Where Do We Go?*, Billie Eilish stated that Ariana 'deserved [the award] more than anything in the world'.[10]

One of the most impressive things about *Thank U,*

*Next* and its success is how effortless and off-the-cuff Grande made it seem. Like, *yes, I've just made the best album of my career and am now the biggest pop star in the world. So what?*

Following on from the record's rapturous reception, Grande finally made good on her promise to tour – hitting the road with the Sweetener Tour, with a setlist that combined most of the tracks from both *Sweetener* and *Thank U, Next*. She ticked a big A-list pop star wish off by headlining the 2019 Coachella Festival and also returned to the city of Manchester for the first time in two years for a surprise headline slot at Manchester Pride.

But being so candid on *Thank U, Next* would have its consequences. I wouldn't call Ariana overexposed at the end of 2019, but she was certainly heading that way, having made headlines pretty much every week for a straight eighteen months. Even Ariana herself acknowledged that the hurricane of emotion that had birthed *Thank U, Next* had begun to affect her. She memorably candidly told *Vogue* that she 'couldn't remember' most of the recording sessions for the album.

'I don't really remember how it started or finished,' she shared. 'I was so drunk and so sad. I think that this is the first album and also the first year of my life where I'm realizing that I can no longer put off spending time with myself, just as me.'[11]

It's clear she knew a pause was needed and we do see a distinct pullback from the public eye and a reclamation of her. What no one could predict, however, is just how much privacy Ariana would get in 2020 when the world would shut down for a life-shifting global pandemic.

ARIANA GRANDE

## 'THANK U, NEXT'

**Release date:** 3 November 2018
**Written by:** Ariana Grande, Tayla Parx, Victoria Monét, Tommy Brown, Njomza Vitia, Kimberly Krysiuk, Michael Foster, Charles Anderson
**Produced by:** Tommy Brown, Social House

Ariana Grande lays it all on the line in 'Thank U, Next'. I've talked a lot about authenticity being a huge theme of pop music in the last few years and 'Thank U, Next' is perhaps one of the most authentic and bracingly honest records recorded in recent memory.

Don't believe me? From the first second the song starts playing, Grande reels off the names of her ex-boyfriends with a carefree candour. Big Sean? Not a match. Ricky Alvarez? Inspired some songs, yes, but now they make her laugh. Pete Davidson? They *almost* got married. Mac Miller is only referenced by his first name, Malcolm. Grande calls him an angel and I honest to God think you can hear the sadness in her voice for that one word, which she elongates slightly, her vibrato almost quivering.

'Thank U, Next' isn't meant to make you sit back and reflect on Grande's past relationships with a pensive gaze or analyse them to the nth degree. She doesn't even want you to feel sad or angry for her. Instead, it's a message from her to you: she's suffered, yes. She's hurting, of course. But she's ready to move on.

The magic of 'Thank U, Next' is that it never comes off as accusatory or vindictive. Instead, the story is entirely Grande's and she lets us know that no one but herself is responsible for her own healing. The light, airy production by Brown and Social House helps in that regard; the backing to Grande's words is graceful and slick. It never overpowers her or takes over. Instead, the light strumming of a guitar or the soft ripple of a synthesiser in the background just carry us along, keeping us in time to what she's saying, the sermon she's preaching.

For all the noise of 'Thank U, Next' as the definitive breakup anthem of its generation, the song itself is actually not so concerned at all with Grande's exes. They are named and rolled out only for her to reassure us that, yes, all these relationships were meaningful to her, but they didn't define her. Instead, the core of the song is much more about her own self-acceptance. In the second verse, she casts herself as her *own* love interest, a neat lyrical twist I have appreciated in both this track and 'Liability' by Lorde. She now realises that only *she* is responsible for her own happiness. Anyone who doesn't add to that? Well, they know what to do.

Remember how I said that *Thank U, Next* was written quickly? Well, the lead single came out just over a month after writing had started, but the final version was very much in a state of flux. Given the tumultuous nature of Grande's relationship with Davidson, there were several drafts of his line in the first verse written to accommodate various outcomes, including the couple staying together or breaking up. We now know what happened there but it's fascinating to note that 'Thank U, Next' was being composed in almost real time and what the butterfly effect could have been for the song and its message, had it all worked out another way.

We all know that breakups can be messy, *especially* from comparatively short-term relationships, which have the craziest breakups of them all and this was no exception for Grande and Davidson. Davidson's day job, of course, is a comedian and at the time he was one of the rising stars on US variety show *Saturday Night Live* and suddenly, thanks to his new-found fame, one of its biggest draws. On 2 November 2018, during a promo shot for that Saturday's forthcoming live episode, Davidson joked about his failed engagement to Grande and pretended to propose instead to that week's musical guest, Maggie Rogers.

As you can imagine, this did not go down well. Grande, furious, tweeted lyrics to a then-unnamed track we now know as 'Thank U, Next'. The next day, about thirty minutes before *Saturday Night Live* came to air and with no prior announcement, she surprise-released the track in full. Although you will be glad to know, apparently she previewed the track for both Big Sean and Ricky Alvarez to get their blessings and even informed Davidson himself of the impending release. Davidson, for what it's worth, then asked permission from the show's producer, Lorne Michaels, to axe a previously written sketch about his and Grande's relationship.

It is, of course, the goal of every pop star to have a Number 1 hit (at least *I* think so; anyone who says otherwise is lying). You can't say that, up until this point, Ariana hadn't given it the good college try. However, good things come to those who wait and I don't think anyone could argue that even though she had to wait a while longer than some of her contemporaries like Taylor Swift ('We Are Never Ever Getting Back Together' in 2012) or Miley Cyrus ('Wrecking Ball' in 2013), 'Thank U, Next's landmark debut at Number 1 in the US in November 2018 was finally the right moment and the right song for her to get her wish. This was no flash-in-the-pan, either. 'Thank U, Next' was at the centre of a viral social media storm and its dominance of headlines and Stan Twitter's timelines resulted in it staying at Number 1 for a total of seven weeks.

During its long reign at Number 1 on the Billboard Hot 100, Grande also debuted 'Thank U, Next's music video. I don't think anyone can argue against it being her greatest visual achievement. Sidestepping the tragic undertones of the song, she and director Hannah Lux Davis instead used the video to pay homage to several iconic teen movies of the early 2000s: *Mean Girls, Bring It On, 13 Going On 30* and *Legally Blonde*.

Whether she was pouting to the camera as Regina George or vamping down the driveway as Elle Woods, Ariana is the main draw of the video, mustering all of her star power (and, it must be said, a very good spray tan). Watching the 'Thank U, Next' video is also great because of the many, many cameos throughout, including but not limited to, Jennifer Coolidge reprising her role from *Legally Blonde* (this would be the start of a career renaissance for Coolidge, culminating in her award-winning role in *The White Lotus* a few years after 'Thank U, Next' brought her back into the cultural conversation), Troye Sivan being shoved up against a locker or Kris Jenner referencing Amy Poehler's ultimate 'cool mom' from *Mean Girls*. *Victorious* fans also got a look-in too – with 'Thank U, Next' reuniting Grande on-screen with former co-stars Liz Gillies, Matt Bennett and Daniella Monét.

The world was ready and waiting for the 'Thank U, Next' video. With 55.4 million views within its first day, it became for a time the most-watched music video on the platform in twenty-four hours. Its all-time views currently stand at 856 million. Very fetch!

And it wasn't just fans or the critics, but Grande's peers who reacted to this major moment. Justin Bieber once memorably named 'Thank U, Next' as a 'bop. It's my favourite song.'[12] Billie Eilish claimed Grande's voice was 'fucking crazy' in an interview, adding, 'Can you imagine opening your mouth and *that* comes out? Holy fuck!'[13]

Even Lana Del Rey, the patron saint of cool indie girls, was gagging. '"Thank U, Next" came out and I freaking loved that record. Every song [was so good] I was like, "how did she write that?"'[14]

Having waited half a decade for her first chart-topper,

Ariana's next one would come almost immediately, for a song completely different to 'Thank U, Next' in almost every conceivable way possible.

## '7 RINGS'

**Release date:** 18 January 2019
**Written by:** Ariana Grande, Tayla Parx, Victoria Monét, Tommy Brown, Michael Foster, Charles Anderson, Njomza Vitia, Kimberly Krysiuk, Richard Rodgers, Oscar Hammerstein II
**Produced by:** Tommy Brown, Social House

'My dream has always been to be obviously not to be a rapper, but, like, to put out music in the way that a rapper does,' so Ariana Grande said in a big, splashy cover story with *Billboard* in 2018. 'I just want to fucking talk to my fans and sing and write music and drop it the way these boys do. Why do they get to make records like that and I don't?'[15]

On the braggadocious, slyly hilarious '7 rings', Ariana not only did just that, but for a brief moment at least, she doesn't just emulate 'the boys', she *becomes* one of them.

The one thing I've come to love about '7 rings' – the one song that, perhaps, stands out like a sore thumb on *Thank U, Next* – is that you can only truly appreciate what Grande is trying to do here when you realise you shouldn't be taking anything she says seriously.

Hip-hop has always played a part in her music. She has engaged with the genre mostly by welcoming some of its bastions as guest stars into her world but it was no great surprise when these influences, which had existed mostly as subtext, came fully to the forefront on '7 rings'.

To call '7 rings' an out-and-out rap song would be a lie, though. It's definitely emulative of the rap sub-genre trap, which was undergoing something of a resurgence at the time. Childish Gambino's first and only US Number 1 hit, 'This Is America', built much of its production around trap beats and trap played a huge part in the birth of 'mumble rap', whose rise was attributed to SoundCloud rappers Lil Peep and Juice WRLD.

I wouldn't exactly call Ariana *rapping* on this song, but it's close enough. The verses – all about the wealth she has accrued and the power she now holds – are clearly meant to mirror the structure of a rap song. But you also can't ignore the tight melodies and pop sheen running through the entire thing – because we haven't talked about the Maria von Trapp of it all.

'7 rings' does have heavy trap influences, yes, but its other big inspiration is a little different. Did someone say . . . *The Sound of Music*? Yes, for this track all about the finer things in life, Grande pulled from the canon of musical theatre for one of the most famous songs about indulgence. 'My Favorite Things' was written by the legendary duo Rodgers and Hammerstein (Richard Rodgers and Oscar Hammerstein II) for inclusion in *The Sound of Music*. Its most famous iteration, of course, is the 1966 live-action film, starring Julie Andrews as Maria, a nun-turned-nanny for the wealthy von Trapp family during the outbreak of World War II in Austria.

In the film, 'My Favorite Things' most famous placement is during the second act of the film, where Maria encourages the von Trapp children to think of their favourite things whenever they are feeling down.

Grande's wish-list isn't *quite* so wholesome. In fact, a list of her favourite things includes the titular seven rings, objects which were the genesis of her second Number 1 hit. The story goes that one day during the initial two-week recording sessions for *Thank U, Next*, she took several of her collaborators (Victoria Monét, Tayla Parx, Njomza Vitia and Kimberly Krysiuk) and two of her childhood friends (Courtney Chiponle and Alexa Luria) to Tiffany's, the famous New York boutique jewellery store, for a bit of retail therapy. While there, Grande was served a lot of champagne by eager shopping assistants and decided not to just buy one Tiffany ring for herself, but an additional six too.

'7 rings' is definitely materialistic; Grande admits she accumulates all these expensive things *because* of her wealth. But there's a deeper, sadder reading to the song too. Underneath all the braggadocious lyricisms and trap beats, she knows, in her heart, that no matter how many rings or red bottoms she buys herself, she's not going to fix the crack in her heart. But she's drunk, she's upset, and she keeps going, because healing doesn't happen in a straight line and everyone's journey is different.

With a bit of space from the song's release, we know that material things don't *really* matter to Grande. She's never made another song like '7 rings'. Instead, we see the actions of someone with all the money in the world and no idea what to do or how to fix herself. When you think about it like that, it's hard not to feel sorry for her – drunk in Tiffany's, desperately trying to buy her way out of pain.

For a song all about opulence and success, there is a touch of irony that the most expensive thing about '7 rings' is its sample. A few weeks out from the song's debut, Grande's label reached out to the estates of Rodgers and Hammerstein, seeking permission to use the sample of 'My Favorite Things' (Richard Rodgers died in 1979, Oscar Hammerstein II in 1960).

According to the *New York Times*, Concord Music – a publishing company that has owned the rights to the duo's catalogue since 2017 – listened to '7 rings' and told Republic Records they would clear the sample . . . for 90 per cent of the publishing rights.[16] This kind of split is unbelievably rare but speaks to how important the sample was not only to the structure but the intent behind '7 rings'. Grande, who was really backed into a corner with the song only weeks away from release, could do nothing but accept. The *NYT* also notes, however, that while most of the songwriting profits of '7 rings' go directly to Rodgers and Hammerstein, Grande will also make royalties through being the track's performer.

With such a hefty price tag, '7 rings' more than justified the cost. It was an instant success, debuting at Number 1 on the Billboard Hot 100. This was Grande's second consecutive Number 1 hit and she was the third female artist ever, after Mariah Carey and Britney Spears, to have multiple songs debut at Number 1.

'7 rings', no doubt benefitting from the significant hype that followed the release of 'Thank U, Next' and continued to build up to the album proper, is Ariana's biggest chart-topping hit by some margin. It spent a total of eight weeks at Number 1 and was eventually certified as a Diamond record by the RIAA (Recording Industry Association of America). In the UK, it also debuted at Number 1 on the Official Singles Chart, Grande's fourth Number 1 hit there, and actually at the time broke the record for the most number of streams received by a song in a single week, with 16.9 million.[17]

I'd say that was worth the hefty price tag.

GEORGE GRIFFITHS

## 'BREAK UP WITH YOUR GIRLFRIEND, I'M BORED'

**Release date:** 8 February 2019
**Written by:** Ariana Grande, Max Martin, Ilya, Savan Kotecha, Kandi Burruss, Kevin Briggs
**Produced by:** Max Martin, Ilya

'Break Up with Your Girlfriend, I'm Bored' is the final track on *Thank U, Next*, although that wasn't always supposed to be the plan. The record was originally meant to be closed with a track called 'reMeMbr', but it was removed from the track list at the last moment by Grande herself, who found the subject matter too personal – it's heavily rumoured to be a tribute to Mac Miller.

'Break Up with Your Girlfriend, I'm Bored' uses a sample of 'It Makes Me Ill' by early '00s boyband *NSYNC. Max Martin, the song's producer and co-writer, was famously responsible for some of *NSYNC's greatest hits, such as 'It's Gonna Be Me', but ironically, he had nothing to do with 'It Makes Me Ill'. The song's original writers, Kandi Burruss (legendary hitmaker for '90s classics like 'Bills Bills Bills' by Destiny's Child and TLC's 'No Scrubs') and Kevin 'She'kspere' Briggs are credited on 'Break Up with Your Girlfriend, I'm Bored' as a result.

Personal relationships can be nebulous and knotted, but if you can't guess it from the title, Ariana doesn't care about that – she's going to take what she wants, when she wants it. I don't know if this is obvious to *everyone*, but please do not take this song seriously. Instead, I always read it as Ariana coming into a place of extreme confidence after all she's endured. At the end of *Thank U, Next* she's comfortable with herself again, finally. She knows what she's worth. So, do you *really* want her that badly? Then you have to break up with your girlfriend before you can even *entertain* the idea. Grande's tongue is firmly in her cheek here; you can almost feel the cheeky glint in her eyes as she glides through Max Martin and Ilya's trap-infused pop beats, all stark clicks and a deep, booming bass, carrying you off into your deepest, darkest desires.

These deep, dark desires are expanded upon no end in the track's equally knotty video, once again directed by Hannah Lux Davis. We catch up with Grande as she attends a party deep in the Hollywood hills. She catches the attention of a very handsome guy (*Riverdale* star and future *May December* standout Charles Melton) but wouldn't you know it, he has a girlfriend. But wait . . . doesn't his girlfriend (played by the model Ariel Yasmine) look a lot like Ariana Grande herself?

There was some controversy around the clip when it was first released. The big twist ending sees Grande reject Melton's character and sidle on over to his girlfriend, her own doppelganger, in a hot tub. They both lean in and the camera cuts to black. Some critics accused Grande of queerbaiting ('queerbaiting' is the act of hinting at the inclusion of queer narratives or character in a body of work, intentionally baiting LGBTQ+ audiences into watching and ultimately not including them) given that we never *actually* see the two female characters kiss. I understand the need to signal this as queerbaiting - God knows we need more queer narratives, voices and characters represented in all media – but I don't think that's actually the point of the clip. The girlfriend is a reflection of Grande herself – she could even act as a visual metaphor *for* Grande.

The hinted-at kiss at the end, therefore, is in my eyes an act of narcissism on Grande's behalf and very much in keeping with the thesis of much of *Thank U, Next*. She doesn't want, or need, the validation of a man each and every time now. Just like in the album's title track, now she will choose herself.

'Break Up with . . .' was released in tandem with the rest of the *Thank U, Next* album on 8 February 2019. It debuted and peaked at Number 2 on the Billboard Hot 100, being blocked by Grande's own '7 rings', with 'Thank U, Next' following up at Number 3. That made history. Ariana was officially the first female artist to hold the Top 3 positions at the same time in the same week and only the second act ever after The Beatles – you know a record's good when the only other act to have done it is the Fab Four themselves.

It went one further in the UK, becoming Grande's fifth Number 1 single, replacing her own '7 rings' in the top spot. That, again, was history; Grande was the first female artist to replace herself at Number 1 on the UK

Singles Chart and only the second female artist to hold the Top 2 positions consecutively, since Madonna in 1985.

To have this amount of success with three successive singles is, actually, not common. Pop campaigns are usually front-loaded with the first big hit before other releases in the schedule usually dwindle in its wake. This is clearly not the case with Ariana Grande or with *Thank U, Next*. The album was turning out hit after hit, reaching record-breaking streaming numbers and helping her establish herself as an out-and-out superstar. These sort of success stories do not happen overnight and Grande's imperial phase wasn't built in a day. It was the result of years and years of hard work and determination, of some truly brilliant pop music and finding the right audience for it to connect with.

Sadly, though, no imperial phase can last forever.

## 'DON'T CALL ME ANGEL' with Miley Cyrus and Lana Del Rey

**Release date:** 13 September 2019
**Written by:** Ariana Grande, Miley Cyrus, Lana Del Rey, Max Martin, Savan Kotecha, Ilya, ALMA
**Produced by:** Ilya, Max Martin

As 2019 was drawing to a close, so too was the *Thank U, Next* era. It had made Ariana Grande, by any reasonable metric, the most famous and successful pop star in the world. Most of the year, post-release, would be spent in preparation and rehearsal for the Sweetener Tour – Grande's first live touring show in two years. The Sweetener Tour ran from March to December 2019, and while she wasn't actively working on new music for her own projects during this time, Ariana did find time to diversify.

She guested on production duo Social House – who had helped produce both 'Thank U, Next' and '7 rings' – on their debut artist single, 'Boyfriend', a Top 10 hit in the US, but her biggest new project came in the form of the curation of the *Charlie's Angels* soundtrack.

The 2000 *Charlie's Angels* film starring Cameron Diaz, Lucy Liu and Drew Barrymore famously had Destiny's Child's timeless classic 'Independent Women, Part 1' on its soundtrack, so expectations for what Ariana Grande could achieve in 2019 were high. When it was announced that she would collaborate with both Miley

Cyrus and Lana Del Rey on 'Don't Call Me Angel', I did for a brief moment think we were approaching the release of possibly the greatest song ever made.

Spoiler alert: we weren't! My main issue with 'Don't Call Me Angel' is that it feels incredibly rushed. It has the distinction of being over-thought and under-baked. Grande, Cyrus and Del Rey are not only three very different artists but three very different *singers*. There is, in some alternate timeline, a way to interrogate their personas (and voices) and find a through-line for a more cohesive song. Sadly, this didn't happen. Each artist takes a chunk separately – Cyrus the first verse, Grande the chorus and the second verse, and Del Rey the bridge. This doesn't help the cobbled-together feel (one can only assume they were working on a very tight deadline to write, release and record the song to promote the film).

Now, Cyrus and Grande's verses do at least seem like they were written for the same song (and Max Martin *does* sample the theme song from the *Charlie's Angels* TV song in the production so at least it's on brand!), although Grande's verses seem uncharacteristically under-written, most of them comprised of the same three lines, just repeated until the chorus comes back again. Her heart just doesn't seem in it!

Del Rey's bridge *is* the best and most distinctive portion of 'Don't Call Me Angel', even if it *does* sound like she's just been blasted in from a completely different song. It's like Martin and Ilya have to bend the entire world of the song to accommodate her presence. As you should! Whereas 'Independent Women, Part I' was a rallying call to arms for unity and feminist strength, none of 'Don't Call Me Angel's many differing parts ever work in harmony. There's no soul there. The chorus, at least, has the beginnings of a good idea of interrogating what an 'angel' is, but this throughline is never followed through in any meaningful way.

The song as it stood wasn't a massive success, either. After a bunch of hype leading up to the release, 'Don't Call Me Angel' debuted at a somewhat disappointing Number 13 in the US. A sign, perhaps, that Ariana Grande's imperial phase was waning since she had previously seemed to walk to a few Number 1 debuts with no difficulty, although it did perform very well in the UK, reaching Number 2. Somewhat depressingly, it is still Del Rey's highest-charting single in the UK.

Grande gifts just one solo track to the *Charlie's Angels* soundtrack, but 'How I Look On You' might just be one of her most underrated tracks ever. A stuttering, dark-pop track built around an ominous guitar bass and shattering trap beats, it's a thinly veiled response-track to a former partner who she fears was just using her for her fame. It's one of her most bracingly honest tracks and could have slotted in very easily on the track list to *Thank U, Next*. To me, there is no greater compliment!

'Don't Call Me Angel' would be the last we would hear from Grande in a while. Focused on the Sweetener Tour, the aftermath of the *Thank U, Next* era we can see her purposefully pulling away from living such a public life – and who could blame her?

In fact, for her next era, Ariana would conduct her new relationship with her future husband in almost total secrecy – and during one of the darkest times in modern history – returning with a pop smash so joyous and victorious, it helped wash away your tears in the rain.

# 7
# *Positions*, Marriage and 'Rain On Me'

No one was prepared for 2020.

The start of the COVID-19 pandemic was a destabilising and genuinely unprecedented time. For a moment, you might be forgiven for wondering if anything would ever be the same again. Among all the death and the chaos, however, there was one thing during the pandemic and the subsequent lockdowns that could be looked on as a positive: giving people the opportunity, for the first time in years, to sit back and reflect. To realign and reaffirm what they wanted to do with their lives.

As far as I can tell, Ariana Grande had no active plans to record new music at the start of the year. With 2019 had ended both the Sweetener World Tour, which has been, to date, her last world tour – she's thrown doubt on the prospect of another but has hinted she could tour on a smaller scale in the near future – and the promotional run for *Thank U, Next*. Grande had released two studio albums within twelve months of each other and she had seen her celebrity balloon to almost unimaginable heights.

One of her last public appearances before the world shut down was at the 2020 Grammy Awards. She walked the record carpet in a stunning Giambattista Valli grey ballgown that was 90 per cent ruffle, dyeing her signature ponytail a blonde ombre, before taking to the stage to perform a mash-up of 'Imagine', '7 rings' and 'Thank U, Next' to rapturous applause. It was a reminder of just *how* big she had become, just how much her star had been shot into the stratosphere.

*Thank U, Next* must have been exhausting for Grande, both emotionally while making the album, physically while promoting it and mentally, reckoning with the fallout of the overwhelming media interest in her and her personal life.

Some pop stars relish this attention and can build careers around it. Taylor Swift, for example, has been canny in using the media attention in her relationships and personal life to sharply critique perceptions of her and to even parody her own man-eating persona in songs like 'Blank Space'. For Ariana Grande, though, it seemed once was enough. When she met the LA-based realtor Dalton Gomez in January 2020, their courtship was not announced publicly and she was savvy enough to keep all personal details scrubbed from her social media. This time, she would fall in love *away* from the cameras.

As the world locked down, she hunkered down in LA and, with considerable time on her hands, began to secretly work on new music. Slowly but surely, the pieces would come together for her sixth album, *Positions*.

*Positions* is a pointed return to the R&B-focused sonics of her debut, *Yours Truly*, and away from the pop sheen that had dominated some of her biggest hits up until this point. It was a long time coming. In a *Vogue* cover story the previous year, she had opened up candidly about a 'two-album period' that I would guess is highly likely to be *My Everything* to *Dangerous Woman*, where she had to make serious concessions to further her career.

'I was doing half the songs for me and half the songs to solidify my spot in pop music,' she told *Vogue*. 'A lot of my singles have been hilariously lacking in substance. You're talking to someone who put *Side to Side* out as a single. I love that song, but it's just a fun song about sex.'[1]

*Positions* is, front to back, exactly the kind of album Ariana needed to make at this moment in her life. Instead of trying to live up to matching the hype and success of the blockbuster, *Thank U, Next*, she in fact relishes the challenge of doing the exact opposite. There is no 'one for me, one for them' mindset here and no tracks clearly nestled into the track list with the sole intent of being a future radio single. It's telling that *Positions* is the first and only Grande album since *Yours Truly* not to include Max Martin in any capacity. Instead, it is more or less an entire record where Ariana, Tommy Brown, Victoria Monét and Tayla Parx can really indulge themselves in lush, grandiose soundscapes and vocals that, at times, verge on heaven-sent melisma.

It's an album full of intent and you could well argue that following on from the biggest commercial success of her career, the release of *Positions* freed Grande from not only the pop star hamster wheel, but also the pressure of trying to beat her previous record-breaking successes. It established her as a true artist, less reliant on hit singles but *still* able to collect number ones like infinity stones. In 2020 alone, she earned three of her nine US Number 1 singles.

*Positions* or *Eternal Sunshine* have not reached the same levels of cultural hegemony as *Thank U, Next* but this reads as an intentional ploy on Grande's part, rather than a sign of any declining cultural capital.

The soundscape of the record is gorgeous. It flows like a pond. Ariana feels more confident, now, in using her voice as an instrument to complement the production of these songs, which gives *Positions* the distinction of functioning, in her biography, as a totally whole concept.

Make no mistake about it, *Positions* is a concept record. The concept at its core is very simple: Ariana is in love again. Because of this, you could very well locate *Positions* as the end statement in a loose trilogy of records beginning with *Sweetener* and continuing in *Thank U, Next*. Together, they track Ariana's journey of healing as a complicated odyssey, full of peaks and troughs and mistakes and relapses. But here, she is more at peace than she's ever sounded. On the opening number, 'Shut

Up', she literally tells us to leave all our baggage and expectations about who she is at the door. Here, she barrels headfirst into a new era of early love and the bliss of the honeymoon period.

Across its luxuriant fourteen tracks containing three initial collaborations with Doja Cat, The Weeknd and Ty Dolla $ign, *Positions* is very patient and purposeful in telling you that Ariana has found quiet joy in her new relationship with Dalton Gomez. But it's not all rosy. She's in love again, yes, but she's also terrified at the prospect of that, of allowing her heart into someone else's hands and getting hurt again. There's a specific tension that powers through *Positions*: *I'm happy now, but will it last?*

We've touched on Ariana's approach to sex in her music. In previous records, sex has been something that has happened in the background ('Love Me Harder') or teased as something that's *about* to happen just as soon as the song has finished ('Into You') or played as some kind of joke ('Side To Side'). *Positions* changes tack completely. Grande tackles the act of sex with a clear-eyed clarity on many of this album's tracks, sometimes even pointing it out full-out ('34+35'), while 'Off The Table' with The Weeknd, 'My Hair' and 'Nasty' seem to channel the queen of the sex jam herself, Janet Jackson.

Grande had emerged from her lockdown cocoon briefly in the summer of 2020 to secure two US Number 1 singles with two very different duets: 'Stuck With U' with Justin Bieber and 'Rain On Me' with Lady Gaga.

Then she disappeared again for a few months. Rumours still abounded that she was working on new music, but it didn't seem ready or in sight. Then, on 14 October 2020, Ariana announced that work had been completed on her sixth album and it would be released the same month. This was a bracingly almost-surprise drop from one of pop's newest superstars and mirrors a similar trick Taylor Swift played when she announced on 23 July 2020 that her eleventh (and best) studio album, *Folklore*, would be released that night.

This decision speaks to how much COVID-19 had levelled the music landscape in 2020. Albums such as Lady Gaga's *Chromatica* or Dua Lipa's *Future Nostalgia* were pushed back initially and many artists had to cancel planned tours or releases due to the spread of the virus. But music is release, and Ariana pushed past any such anxieties and helped us escape with *Positions*, which was released in full on 30 October 2020, a week after its title track (which became her fifth US Number 1 single).

Upon release, *Positions* became Grande's third US Number 1 album in under two years and three months, a record for a female artist at the time and her fifth Number 1 album in her home country.

It is really nice to hear Ariana in such a place of peace and serenity in *Positions*. She would marry Dalton Gomez in a private ceremony at their California home in December 2020, with the couple not announcing their union to the public until May 2021. Grande's Instagram announcement of the wedding, which contains a look at her custom-made wedding dress by Vera Wang, garnered 25 million likes and was briefly the second most-liked Instagram post of all time. It seemed, after all the pain and trauma that she had gone through, she had finally found her happy ending. For a moment, too, it seemed like the door to her music career had been shut for the foreseeable future too, when it was revealed that she would be making her big-screen debut as Glinda the Good Witch in the much-hyped live-action adaptation of the musical *Wicked*, alongside Cynthia Erivo as Elphaba, who eventually becomes the Wicked Witch of the West.

That would not be the case. But Ariana approached her next heartbreak like she had the others – she made a really good album about it.

ARIANA GRANDE

# 'RAIN ON ME' with Lady Gaga

**Release date:** 22 May 2020
**Written by:** Lady Gaga, Ariana Grande, BloodPop, Burns, Nija Charles, Rami, Tchami, Boyz Noise
**Produced by:** BloodPop, Burns

Do you hear that thunder coming down?

During the height of the COVID-19 lockdown, you might be forgiven for thinking that life would never be the same again. Shut in your house with nothing to do, I don't know about you, but one thing that helped me keep my sanity was listening to the most jubilant pop music possible.

'Rain On Me', the chart-topping duet by Lady Gaga and Ariana Grande that helped launch Gaga back to the top tier of the pop pantheon after something of a fallow period, was not originally written or recorded with hindsight of the world-altering events that were to follow, but for many people (myself included), no song seems to encapsulate this period of human history more. 'Rain On Me' was a gift, sent down from the pop heavens and by God, were we thankful for it!

Like the best of Gaga's music, 'Rain On Me' has a rich emotional depth and resonance and Ariana Grande was the perfect partner to bring the song and its message to life. You see, 'Rain On Me' is a song about trauma. Trauma and pain so overwhelming that they threaten to consume and destroy you.

Disco was having a *moment* in 2020, and even though 'Rain On Me' was written and recorded before lockdown, it slotted in neatly with a movement that brought the sub-genre back to commercial prominence, thanks to several global hits: 'Blinding Lights' by The Weeknd, 'Don't Start Now' by Dua Lipa and 'Say So' by Doja Cat. But 'Rain On Me' has something all those other (very good!) songs do not have: Lady Gaga and Ariana Grande meeting on a record for the first time ever. In fact, 'Rain On Me' feels somewhat removed from the early 70's disco boom, instead feeling more indebted to emulating another meeting of iconic divas, Barbra Streisand and the late, great Donna Summer on 1979's 'No More Tears (Enough Is Enough)', of which 'Rain On Me' could very much function as a spiritual sequel.

As mutually beneficial as Grande's inclusion on 'Rain On Me' was from a publicity point of view, it also made perfect sense from a thematic standpoint too. Gaga said as much herself in an interview around the song's release with Zane Lowe on Apple's Beats Radio, where she admitted that Ariana might have expected to just come into the studio, cut lines written for her and call it a day, but Gaga wanted their connection on the song to be much more emotional.

'I asked her what she needed [to say on the song], how she wanted to do things,' Gaga told Lowe. 'When she came to the studio, I was still crying [. . .] she came up to me and said, "you're hiding", and I said, "yeah, you're right, I'm absolutely hiding", and that's where our friendship blossomed.'[2]

You can hear that connection transmitted in real time on the song. Gaga and Grande have a harmony together that is so rare to find when genuine superstars tend to collaborate (which is why it doesn't really happen very much, to be honest). Grande is the tender heart of the track – when she opens up her second verse, the song seems brighter because of it. Rain, in the song, exists as a metaphor for the process of healing. In the most tantalising moment of the song, in the post-chorus that closes the entire thing out, Ariana implores the thunder to roar, to send a flood our way. I genuinely think it was the best bit of any pop song to come out that year.

More fascinating still is the track's music video. It's a visually extravagant feast, helmed by noted film director Robert Rodriguez, who transports Gaga and Grande to a cyber-punk imagined future that's part *Hunger Games*, part *Blade Runner*. Rain and daggers pour down from the thundering sky as Grande appears decked head to toe in futuristic leather and sky-high platforms, looking like a goddess from the Planet Slay. Dancing and choreography have never been her forte, but here in Gaga's world, she commits fully, performing intricate dance moves with a panache and lightness that make you wonder why she wasn't doing this type of stuff before. Seeing her and Gaga, a master of pop performance art, work together is thrilling – they look like they're genuinely having the time of their lives throughout the whole clip.

It's always strange to wonder what might have happened to 'Rain On Me' if it had been released in a normal year, if you could have actually heard it while *out*. But lockdown or no lockdown, it was still a massive success. 'Rain On Me' debuted at Number 1 on the Billboard Hot 100, becoming Grande's fourth chart-topper (she had gained her third just two weeks earlier with the Justin Bieber collaboration, 'Stuck With U' – it is simply not very good) and Gaga's fifth. It also debuted at Number 1 in the UK, obviously. This was pop justice in action!

Lockdown wasn't great for live performances. Large-scale tours were delayed or sometimes cancelled altogether, but there was *one* bright spot: Gaga and Grande did perform 'Rain On Me' live (kind of) for the first and only time at that year's MTV VMAs. The performance formed part of a *Chromatica* medley for Gaga, but space and time are made for a full performance of 'Rain On Me', given its status as the big hit of that era.

It is amazing from start to finish. Masked up, Gaga and Grande gallantly breeze through the song and choreography before the song's outro, where Grande hits an extravagant high whistle note clear enough to crack every glass within 200 yards. When she's done, Gaga looks fit to bursting with pride and whispers something to Grande that we can't hear. What did she say to her? We have been begging for an answer to this immortal question for half a decade. When Gaga was quite literally confronted by one of her Little Monsters during a fan press conference for her new album *Mayhem*, she blanked.

'I have no idea,' she said. 'You'll have to ask Ari.'[3]

Ari, let us know, Queen!

# GEORGE GRIFFITHS

## 'POSITIONS'

**Release date:** 23 October 2020
**Written by:** Ariana Grande, Tommy Brown, Tayla Parx, Nija Charles, Angelina Barrett, Killah B, London on da Track, Mr Franks, James Jarvis
**Produced by:** Tommy Brown, Mr Franks, London on da Track

What does devotion look like to you? To Ariana Grande, it looks like being flexible. Versatile. Open to trying new things.

On the lead track of her sixth album, Grande likens her new, successful relationship with Dalton Gomez to widening her skill set. She's jumping willingly through so many hoops, she's like an Olympian. Not only is she a pop star, but she's also in the kitchen cooking for her man as well as pleasing him in the bedroom. Grande's claim in the track is that she can do it all. She can settle down with her new partner, but also retain her sense of self. She can emulate a more traditional wife model by entering the kitchen, sure, but she's only doing so because she *wants* to, not because she's made to. She's in the glory of the honeymoon period, and she's not afraid to show it.

'I have to remind myself that I need to not put the pressure on myself to out-do what I've already done,' she said in an interview in 2020. 'That's not the point in being an artist. Certain moments that have happened are what they are . . . I have to worry about making *new* moments.[4]

You can feel that release of pressure on this record. 'Positions' is a thing of beauty. Lean and muscular, quick in all the right places. Producers Tommy Brown, London on da Track and Mr Franks fill the song's world with the Latin-esque strums of an acoustic guitar, fit around cracking trap beats and just the sweetest hints of hazy electronica. It's an absolutely gorgeous soundscape, one that fits Grande like a glove, in fact. It's fast, it's light and it's breezy, and I would attest that it's probably the best made-for-radio single of the last half decade. It may not find Ariana returning with an atom bomb of pop dominance but it *does* see her in a position of complete confidence.

This confidence trickled on over to the production of the track itself. Due to the (literally) isolated nature of its creation, Grande was much more hands-on in the studio than she's ever been before. She's credited as the vocal producer on all tracks on the album and you can see her work in action in a behind-the-scenes video posted to YouTube, detailing the making of the title track.

In the booth, you can see Grande trying to create the song's bridge, stumbling on an idea to stack up her vocals so much on the last line that she creates an insanely memorable hook that wasn't there before. Seeing her work through it on real time, to create what I would argue is the best moment of the entire song if not the whole album, is a bit like watching Leonardo da Vinci sketch out the *Mona Lisa*.

The title of the track is a little bit of the joke. When Grande first announced the song and revealed its single cover, an artsy black-and-white photograph shot by Dave Meyers that actually cuts the top part of her face off as she (we think) stares contemplatively at the camera with her bare midriff exposed, you might be forgiven for thinking, well, this song was going to be *smut*. Of course, it's not and I think that's part of the song's charm. It constantly defies our expectations and instead tells a story quickly approaching marital bliss – but don't forget, on Grande's own terms.

You know what else is on Grande's terms in the *Positions* universe? The presidency! I will say, out of all the concepts I had imagined Ariana and director Dave Meyers, working here together for the first time since 'God Is A Woman', going with it was *not*; what if Ariana Grande were the President of the United States? Grande *is* an avowed Democrat, but the *Positions* video seems like less of an overt political statement and more of an extension of the song's thesis. In this new phase in her life, Grande can do anything – even run the country! For what it's worth, in a 2021 interview with *Allure* magazine, she stated it was actually her then husband Dalton Gomez who originally came up with the video concept.[5]

Indeed, we see Grande get into position throughout the video. She's leading press briefings, overseeing

Cabinet meetings (her Cabinet members include her mother, Joan, and two of the song's co-creators, Victoria Monét and Tayla Parx), walking her dogs across the South Lawn and even making some pasta in the White House kitchens! Some nice context for the video is that it was released a few weeks out from the final presidential debate between then-incumbent President Donald Trump and his eventual successor, Joe Biden. Grande seems to be hinting, cannily, that better days are on the horizon, with this vision of an almost utopian, matriarchal Presidency.

As we've already discussed, Ariana had been lying low personally for most of 2020, but it wasn't exactly like she'd been dormant, with two almost back-to-back Number 1 debuts within two weeks of each other earlier in the year. Despite its more low-slung vibe, 'Positions' officially became Grande's fifth US Number 1 single when it debuted at the top of the Billboard Hot 100. She was the first artist since Drake to have three number ones in a single calendar year and was actually the first female act to achieve this since both Rihanna and Katy Perry in 2010. 'Positions' may have only held on to the Number 1 spot for a singular week, before being displaced by 24KGoldn and Iann Diorr's 'Mood', a massive hit boosted by its virality on the then-rapidly expanding video sharing site, TikTok.

## '34+35' with Doja Cat and Megan Thee Stallion

**Release date:** 15 January 2021 (remix)
**Written by:** Ariana Grande, Doja Cat, Megan Thee Stallion, Courageous Herrera, Tommy Brown, Peter Lee Johnson
**Produced by:** Tommy Brown, Peter Lee Johnson

Are you any good at maths? I'm not, but even *I* know what Ariana Grande is talking about on '34+35'.

'34+35', Grande's ode to 69'ing, is the most explicit song about sex in her discography – and also one of her funniest. But the comedy isn't painted in broad, cartoonish strokes like it is on 'Side To Side'; instead it's far more emulative of a wink-wink, nudge-nudge coquettish charm, kind of like a much more explicit Sabrina Carpenter song.

The joke is, of course, that the subject of the song is very easy to work out. Grande is fooling no one here. Even at the end of the song, where she leads us out with a burst of laughter, she tells us what the song is *exactly* about, which *does* rob it of some of its charm.

My favourite thing about '34+35' is how light and airy its production is. Tommy Brown and Peter Lee Johnson give it such a vivacious feel and its levity is actually a perfect complement to the lyrics, which play on this sense of fun. If it had had a more 'serious' sex jam-esque production, say, like Janet Jackson's 'If', I think a little of its heart would have been lost. Grande is happy talking about it because, when she does, it's all constructed like a joke.

Apparently, '34+35' was originally intended to function as the lead single from *Positions*, before wisely being put aside for the title track. I think this was the correct decision, 'Positions' grace and confidence being the perfect lead-in. '34+35' would have been too destabilising a statement to start off with. Given its wholly explicit nature – something which, as we know, Grande had purposefully either ignored or bound up in layers of subtext in previous tracks – it's understandable that she had some considerable nerves about the track's release.

Talking to *The Zach Sang Show* to celebrate the album's release, Ariana did admit that 'my fear since the beginning is that it would distract from the vulnerability and the sweetness that is the rest of the album.'[6] Which, you know, is entirely correct! But one of the winning things about '34+35' is that it *is* a big swing for Grande and it could have gone bad in so many ways; make it *too* explicit and you could simply just put people off; take it as *too* much of a joke and it would come across like an *SNL* parody song. I think she gets the balance right . . . just about.

'34+35' was issued as the next official single from *Positions* but it didn't prove to have the legs of the title track. Upon initial release, the track peaked at Number 8 on the Billboard Hot 100, becoming Ariana's eighteenth Top 10 single. It performed similarly in the UK, entering at Number 9 on the UK's Official Singles Chart, while *Positions* was in the midst of what would become six-week stint at Number 1. Sadly, the song didn't have legs in terms of staying (or even improving) its position in the Top 10. But never fear – there's a remix on the horizon!

By the start of 2021, most people could count Doja Cat and Megan Thee Stallion as two of popular music's biggest breakout stars, both of whom had used the relatively new video sharing platform TikTok to take their careers to the next level. Not to get *too* into it, but lockdown really did help shift the way music was promoted and ingested. The rise of the video-sharing app TikTok represented a fundamental, seismic shift and the music industry is still trying to catch up. Both Doja and Meg embraced TikTok as a platform to promote their music and they reaped the rewards.

Doja and Meg don't add *too* much to '34+35' for the remix to represent anything new (whereas, for example, Beyoncé's presence on Meg's 'Savage' remix constituted the entire song to basically become something new and much more exciting), but they perfectly complement the cheeky vibes present in the original. Doja takes the second verse – her best line references controversial viral rapper Tekashi69 – while Meg takes the third verse, where she too points out the real meaning of the title.

I like '34+35' – I think it says a lot about the confidence Ariana was feeling in herself and her new relationship at the time. That she felt that she could make a song like this, talking about the things that she does, tells me that she feels more comfortable than ever in her own skin and talking about her own experiences. Being in a loving relationship also includes loads of great sex! Who'd have thought?! Sadly, though, as far as *Positions* singles go, '34+35' is the end of the line. The era came to a somewhat confusing end in 2021, whereby Grande just stopped promoting the record.

It turns out, though, that there *had* been more plans on the horizon. In 2024, on an episode of the popular podcast *Las Culturistas*, Ariana told host Bowen Yang (her co-star on *Wicked* – wonder how they secured that booking?!) and Matt Rogers that a cooler reception to *Positions* from audiences and fans alike made her retroactively cancel plans she had already made for the record.

'[In the beginning of the era] I got [the sense that the reaction from fans] was "this is not what we want" vibes. I'm a Cancer, I'm very sensitive. I can remember that [the feedback] put me in a cage, I judged every single piece [of content]. I scrapped so many things I was going to put out [. . .] and now people love it!'[7]

I think Grande is being a bit too harsh on herself here. *Thank U, Next* had been so banger-heavy and so forward-facing that whatever came next was going to disappoint some fans. But that's what I've come to love from *Positions*. This is the sound of an artist who is not chasing anything anymore. There is no 'one for me, one for them' mindset here. As honest and authentic as *Thank U, Next* was, taking you through Ariana's healing process in real time, I think *Positions* is a true measure of the kind of artist she wants to be and the kind of music she wants to make. 'POV', the third single and last single to be released from *Positions*, is the perfect encapsulation of that and this most misunderstood era.

She couldn't know it at the time, of course, but a lot was about to change. In November 2021, Grande was officially cast as Galinda Upland (or Glinda the Good Witch) in the live-action adaptation of the musical *Wicked*, alongside Cynthia Erivo as Elphaba Thropp (or the Wicked Witch of the West). The film would be helmed by director Jon M. Chu (*Crazy Rich Asians*, *In The Heights*) and began filming in England in 2023. This was *big* – Ariana's first, proper leading role in an honest-to-God blockbuster film – and it would demand all her attention and devotion.

Music, it seemed, would have to go on the backburner until she returned from Oz . . .

. . .or would it?

# 8

# Slowing Down, Divorce and *Eternal Sunshine*

Booking *Wicked* was a big deal. Ariana hadn't acted much since her days on *Nickelodeon*, her biggest roles being blink-and-you'd-miss-'em cameos in the aforementioned *Scream Queens* and Adam McKay's 2021 Netflix comedy-drama, *Don't Look Up*.

Her casting had been unveiled at the same time by Cynthia Erivo, by the film's director Jon M. Chu, who posted a video of both stars on a Zoom call with him, finding out they'd been cast as Galinda and Elphaba at the same time. It's a really cute clip and Ariana is clearly *very* overcome with emotion for what, she had been telling the press for years, had been her dream role.

I will go into more specifics around the production and filming of *Wicked* in the next chapter (and I *know* you're holding space for that!), but suffice to say it was a full-time commitment that became even more of a commitment when the decision was made by Chu and the studio financing the film, Universal Pictures, to split

*Wicked* into two parts, a few weeks out from principal photography beginning in London. This was, obviously, partly a cynical cash-grab for the films to make even more money – memorably, both the last films in the *Harry Potter* and *Hunger Games* franchises were split in two to maximise profit. However, the split also made sense from a creative standpoint too. The centrepiece of the musical, 'Defying Gravity', stops the plot stone-dead in its tracks but it wouldn't be as dramatic or heavy for it to happen, say, an hour into a two-and-a-half-hour film. It would kill everything that came after it and you'd have to rush a lot of exposition to get to that point so quickly anyway.

So, yes, Ariana had a lot on her plate. Before the filming of *Wicked* officially commenced, she announced that, given her full-time commitment to the role, she wouldn't be able to record or release any new music until filming had wrapped (it was set to finish in July 2023 after a four-month shoot). However, the 2023 SAG-AFTRA strike (where the US actors' union moved to suspend all practises due to a myriad of disputes, including pay and the inclusion of AI in filming) affected those plans. The longest strike in Hollywood history, it lasted from July to November 2023 and overlapped with the Writers' Guild of America strike of 2023 too, essentially meaning that for a large of portion of 2023, most Hollywood productions were forced to grind to a complete halt.

Most people would probably have taken this chance

to relax and unwind, but as we've seen, Ariana Grande is not like most people.

Monte Lipman, the CEO of Republic Records, once classified Grande's approach to her career: 'Starts and ends with Ariana.'

'She takes on tremendous responsibility,' he once told *Billboard*. 'And isn't afraid to challenge whomever. Some people are intimidated by that, but I encourage it.'[1]

Although you imagine it didn't take much encouragement from anyone for Ariana to get back to work. She was, once more, sailing on tumultuous waters in her personal life and had to process these events the way she always has: by making music about it.

Just before film of *Wicked* was suspended and the SAG-AFTRA strike began in July 2023, the media began to report that Ariana and her husband, Dalton Gomez, were separating after just two years of marriage. These reports were confirmed by Ariana herself when she officially filed for divorce from Gomez in September of that year, citing irreconcilable differences.

Obviously, this caused a media storm, not least because many outlets also began reporting that, following their separation (which began in February 2023), Ariana was now in a new relationship with her *Wicked* co-star, Ethan Slater. Not for the first time in her career, she found her personal life maligned and dissected in the public domain. Therefore, her seventh album, *Eternal Sunshine*, is both a response record to the media circus and an obituary to her marriage. Work on the record began very quickly when she decamped to New York for a few weeks of studio sessions with her frequent collaborators, Max Martin and Ilya, the first time they had been credited on a Grande project since *Thank U, Next*. *Eternal Sunshine* is the only Ariana Grande album not to include contributions from either Tommy Brown or Victoria Monét.

Reunited, they worked quickly, the album being written, produced and recorded between September and December 2023, which is *very* quick work indeed but also understandable, given Grande's unbelievably tight schedule. She would return to London to finish filming on *Wicked* in January 2024.

Perhaps more than any other Ariana Grande record, *Eternal Sunshine* is a true concept album. The title is a direct reference to Michel Gondry's 2004 acclaimed surrealist drama *Eternal Sunshine of the Spotless Mind*, which takes its name from a line in Alexander Pope's 1717 verse poem, *Eloisa to Abelard*:

> *How happy is the blameless vestal's lot!*
> *The world forgetting, by the world forgot.*
> *Eternal sunshine of the spotless mind!*²

Essentially, this is an extended metaphor about the power (and pain) of memory. Pope says that if you could wipe your mind of all the sorrow and heartbreak you've experienced, you would enter a state of untold bliss, the titular eternal sunshine in your now-spotless mind.

Gondry takes this metaphor and runs with it in his film. It follows a former couple, Joel (Jim Carrey) and Clementine (Kate Winslet), who both willingly undergo an experimental surgery whereby their memories of each other are erased, following the breakdown of their relationship.

Ariana is no fool; the title and conceit of this album is a statement of intent. Not so much a record of 'divorce' as a record of acceptance and release, *Eternal Sunshine* concerns itself entirely with the breakdown of her marriage and the start of her new relationship. It's fertile ground and she found the perfect collaborators in Martin and Ilya, two producers who took her pain and grief and turned it into some of the most glittering, if not melancholic, electronic pop music she has ever put her name to.

Make no mistake about it, though – no one is in the driver's seat here but Ariana. Everything Martin and Ilya do in this record is in complete service of her vision. When you glance at the linear notes of *Eternal Sunshine*'s track list you will notice one thing glaring out at you: Ariana Grande is not only the credited lyricist for every track on the album and in some cases, she is the *only* lyricist, but as a producer too. When she first started working with Max Martin, it was clear that she had to sacrifice a bit of control over the songs they made together, such is the deal you make when you're a hot young star on the rise and you're working with the biggest pop producer of all time. But now, ten years removed from that, there is no such sacrifice being made.

Instead, *Eternal Sunshine* stands as a testament to how much Grande's relationship with Martin and his song factory has evolved; working with her, there is no longer a math problem to decode. She is both the sum and the solution.

Despite it basically functioning as a stopgap in her schedule, *Eternal Sunshine* is an essential Ariana Grande album. You can really tell that, in those quick few weeks that Ariana, Martin and Ilya were working in New York, she had really taken everything she had learnt from every single one of her prior albums and applied those lessons here.

Yes, she plays the hits. Singles like 'Yes, And?' and 'The Boy Is Mine' function as the kind of out-and-out bangers that some fans clearly thought a record like *Positions* lacked. But there are moments of deep introspection, such as in 'We Can't Be Friends (Wait For Your Love)', a truly surprising yet gladly received twist from her, lacquered with so many layers of gorgeous melodies you can't help but dance, even if you have tears in your eyes. It's some of her most accomplished and mature material and the ultimate testament to Grande's vision that, despite being put together in just a few short weeks, it remains one of her most cohesive records, both conceptually and sonically.

A question on the lips of many pop fans in 2024 was, do we count *Eternal Sunshine* as a success? From an artistic point of view, yes. But the commercial reception is a bit more complicated. Yes, both 'Yes, And?' and 'We Can't Be Friends (Wait For Your Love)' both debuted at Number 1 in the US – but they only spent a single week at the top of the charts and didn't have any of the longevity of 2024's biggest hits like Billie Eilish's 'Birds Of A Feather' or Chappell Roan's 'Good Luck, Babe!' Their chart-topping status is more a sign of Grande's front-loaded streaming success, whereby fans, both passive and active, will stream her newest song a lot in the first week but then drop off. This is a common problem in the streaming era, where there are just *so many songs* being released each week, it's hard for a track to achieve any real long-term success.

Upon debut, *Eternal Sunshine* entered in at Number 1 on the Billboard 200 with 227,000 units, including 194.92 million streams. It was Ariana's sixth US Number 1 album and her third-best opening week numbers following *Thank U, Next* (360,000) and *Sweetener* (231,000). *Eternal Sunshine* also debuted at Number 1 in the UK. So, yes, it *was* a success, but not a blockbuster, runaway hit.

*Eternal Sunshine* was never meant to bring her back on top in terms of ultimate pop dominance, but in a calendar year where bracingly authentic and audacious statements from pop's middle-class – Charli xcx's *Brat* and Chappell Roan's *The Rise and Fall Of A Midwest Princess* – it slots right in with the changing tides. But *Eternal Sunshine*, for all its positives, didn't have the sticking power of *Brat*, say (mostly due to the fact that Grande had to stop promoting it to begin promoting *Wicked* and then got swept up in Oscar campaigning) but still proved that she was not done being a pop star. Not by a long shot.

ARIANA GRANDE

## 'SAVE YOUR TEARS' with The Weeknd

**Release date:** 23 April 2021
**Written by:** The Weeknd, Ariana Grande, Max Martin, Oscar Holter, Belly, DaHeala
**Produced by:** Max Martin, Oscar Holter, The Weeknd, Ariana Grande

The last time Ariana Grande collaborated with The Weeknd, in 2014, he was a boundary pushing one-to-watch in search of a breakout moment. When the two decided to work together again in 2021, The Weeknd was the biggest pop star in the world.

With hindsight, it's amazing to see how 'Love Me Harder' captured these two artists, who were both on the verge of superstardom, existing in the same moment, before they got swept away in the hurricane of celebrity. When The Weeknd appeared as a featured guest on the *Positions* track, 'Off The Table', it seemed like a nice call-back to their initial meeting and representative of the massive growth both artists had undergone since then.

It turns out, The Weeknd and Grande's partnership was so harmonious, they didn't want the fun to stop. Months out from the single's initial launch, the two artists began to tease a brand-new collaboration together in April 2021. This was, of course, finally unveiled to be a remix of 'Save Your Tears', now featuring Grande.

The best thing about the remix is that it really opens the world of the song by recasting it as a duet. Grande adds her own verse and pre-chorus, presumably written from the point-of-view of the girl The Weeknd was pleading to in the original. Because, it turns out, they're both as bad as each other. Grande sounds sublime on this remix, her vocals coming in as sweet as honey and in a lower register than we've come to expect from her. Here, she takes The Weeknd's cold taunts and turns them back on him. Maybe, she ponders, *she* was the one who was too flippant with him, that she pushes him away so he can leave, and she doesn't have to run away like she has in the past. It's a complicated situation and the song notably doesn't absolve anyone of guilt.

Also, if you will, look at those credits – where Grande is credited as both a co-writer *and* producer on the remix. It turns out that her affinity for at-home vocal mixing on *Positions* got her interested in doing more. The production does differ in subtle ways from the original – it sounds, at points, hazier, the vocals less clear than previously, highlighting the blurred boundaries and emotions we've stepped into.

The Weeknd truly went to bat for Grande's skills in the studio too. On Twitter, he called her a 'beast' on the production software Pro Tools, while another producer, Kenny Beats, agreed that she was 'insane' at comping her own vocals.[3]

With the combined might of both The Weeknd and Grande, 'Save Your Tears' was a success. The remixed version of the song debuted at Number 1 on the Billboard Hot 100 – it was both artists' sixth chart-topper in the

US. Sadly, we never got a video (just an animated lyric video which no one wants to waste their time watching, right?) but the pair *did* perform their remix live once: at the 2021 iHeartRadio Music Awards. The tension and chemistry between both The Weeknd and Grande is palpable and her vocals are truly heaven-sent here. She absolutely *nails* a whistle note towards the end of the song – she does it so well, it truly takes your breath away.

But it turns out, they weren't just done there! We have one final collaboration between the pair to make note of: in 2023, Grande hopped on a surprise release of The Weeknd's 'Die For You'. 'Die For You' is an interesting case because it was originally released in 2016 as part of The Weeknd's *Starboy* album (this is my favourite Weeknd album by a country mile), but got a second wind, thanks to TikTok. Grande apparently worked on the remix (in which, again, she is credited as both co-writer and producer) while actively filming *Wicked* in London. Again, the song and their pairing proved to be a massive success and it debuted at Number 1 in the US.

Given Grande's comments about her commitment to *Wicked*, many people thought 'Die For You' would be the last Number 1 single she gave us for quite a while but, as it turns out, we didn't really have that long to wait. Less than a year later, she would be back on top with a tantalisingly expressive dance track, batting away media speculation.

## 'YES, AND?'

**Release date:** 12 January 2024
**Written by:** Ariana Grande, Max Martin, Ilya
**Produced by:** Ariana Grande, Max Martin, Ilya

Sorry, did you have something to add?

'Yes, And?' is a welcome return to the dancefloor for Grande after a self-imposed exile. Like all the best dance music, though, this isn't a song *entirely* focused on making you dance to a groove. It has something to say, and someone to say it too.

Following the breakdown of her marriage to Dalton Gomez, it came as some surprise that Ariana had struck up a relationship with her *Wicked* co-star Ethan Slater. Much like her time with Gomez, she has never commented publicly on her relationship with Slater, the actors have never posted about each other on any social media or even attended a red-carpet event officially together.

However, their silence on the rumours has not come without its challenges. Slater's now, ex-wife, Dr Lilly Jay, wrote about both her divorce and her former husband's new relationship with Grande in a personal essay for *The Cut*, published in December 2024, just after the theatrical release of *Wicked*.

'I never thought I would get divorced,' Jay writes. 'Especially not after just giving birth to my first child and especially not in the shadow of my husband's new relationship with a celebrity.'[4]

Jay never definitively comments on Grande and Slater's relationship but does more or less confirm that the breakdown of her marriage occurred while *Wicked* was filming in London.

'My entire adult life, I feared that loss of control and postpartum depression would destroy me,' she wrote. 'One day in London, I looked up and found that they had both arrived.'

In fact, the only confirmation of Ariana's relationship from her own camp came from brother, Frankie Grande, who said in 2024: 'Ethan's a wonderful guy [. . .] all I want is for my sister to be happy. So, if she's happy, I'm happy.'[5]

But Ariana doesn't need to comment publicly because she's made her feelings around her new relationship pretty clear. 'Yes, And?' functions as a vehicle for her to address all the speculation in a way that feels comfortable for her without ever definitely revealing *anything*. Instead, all the emotion in the track – all of Ariana's ire – is directed towards one thing in particular: the media. Now, most pop stars go through a phase where, after reaching the zenith of their celebrity, they make a song about their relationship with the press, like Britney Spears' 'Piece Of Me' or Cardi B's 'Press'. These songs never paint the media in a positive light and after what these women have gone through, why should they? But in more cases than not, response tracks give disenfranchised females the chance to speak out, to shout above the parapet and address things in their own voice, on their own terms.

This in itself is empowering. And the thing is, Grande, like Spears before her, owes us *nothing*. She doesn't have to tell us *anything* if she doesn't want to. But being in the centre of a media storm is hard work. Give too much information and you risk threatening your own internal life; too little and you'll be accused of leading your audience up the garden path.

I think 'Yes, And?' is a perfect response from Ariana because the information she gives us here is purposefully sparse but loaded with meaning. She's much more concerned with telling us how all of this has made her *feel* – and how she's moved past it. Her way of dealing with the constant pressure and scrutiny? Put your lipstick on, she tells us. That fire that threatens to consume you? You can do nothing but walk through it. Embrace the flames. Keep moving, with your eyes on what's next. And if anyone has anything to say to you . . . yes, and?

Grande enunciates the song's title with such *verve*, you can almost see the sarcasm rolling off her tongue. It's both an answer and an invitation. Oh, you want to ask me something? Go on, I dare you. She's staring you down until you blink first.

Sonically, we're in new territory for Grande too. 'Yes, And?' is not a full-on disco song, but it does heavily incorporate handbag house, a sub-genre of house music that exploded in queer nightlife in the '90s (a great early example of handbag house, or diva house as it's sometimes called, being Madonna's 'Vogue'). 'Yes, And?' is all stabbing synths and sharp piano chords over deep, rollicking house beats. It's all tied together, of course, by Grande's vocal performance. Light and airy, yes, but also full of conviction and sarcasm. In a way, the entire song is a joke because she's turning all the speculation of her personal life into nothing more than a punchline.

Grande loads 'Yes, And?' with just enough personal information to make it so specifically her but enough to never reveal the full truth. Here, also, is the perfect example of how her relationship with Max Martin has grown too. If she had made 'Yes, And?' a few years earlier with him, maybe Martin's 'pop math' would be more prevalent but here, there's a fluidity to everything. On tracks like 'Problem' or even 'Into You', you can hear Martin's 'melodic math' hard at work. Each verse, pre-chorus, chorus and bridge sound markedly different from each other and usually involve the twisting of the main melody and hook. On 'Yes, And?', though, the verses lead very easily into the chorus without much discernment. Again, you can *feel* Grande in the driver's seat here. She wasn't calling up Martin and Ilya to surrender herself for another Number 1 hit; instead she's using them to help *her* construct a pop diva dance banger in her own image.

Of course, post *Thank U, Next*, Ariana's artistry is compounded by truth and honesty, especially in her lyrics. When the beat drops for the song's spoken word chorus, she asks us to *not* comment on her body. This was a direct response to comments by both media publications and fans online dissecting her noticeably thinner frame although lest we forget, she had been in training for *Wicked*, an extremely choreography-heavy role. Most musical theatre roles require the constitution of an athlete. Ariana's changed appearance can also be attributed to her decision to stop any cosmetic procedures. In an interview with *Vogue*, she stated publicly for the first time that she had stopped using lip filler in 2018 and had subsequently stopped using fillers and Botox in her face.[6]

In a TikTok video posted to her official account in 2024, Grande said that vocal critics of her appearance were 'comparing my current body [. . .] to the unhealthiest version of my body.'

She admitted that during the *Thank U, Next* era specifically, she 'was on a lot of antidepressants and drinking on them and eating poorly and at the lowest point of my life when I looked the way you consider my healthy, but that in fact wasn't my healthy.'[7]

As we've touched on previously, Grande has never centred choreography or dancing as one of the defining traits of her artistry. *But* things are clearly very different here in the music video for 'Yes, And?'. Emboldened by the intricate dance routines that she had been trained in on the set of *Wicked*, Grande proves herself to be a dedicated and fluid dancer on the 'Yes, And?' video, which sees her and a troupe of dancers performing for and winning over a crowd of critics, before turning to stone.

Given that we were hearing from Grande a lot sooner than many had expected, 'Yes, And?' made an immediate impression. It became her eighth US Number 1 hit and her third consecutively following on from the remixes of 'Save Your Tears' and 'Die For You' with The Weeknd. 'Yes, And?' only managed a week at the top, but it did get a brief boost less than a month later due to the release of a remix featuring none other than Mariah Carey herself! The Elusive Chanteuse and Grande had collaborated in the past (notably on Carey's festive single, 'Oh Santa!' with Jennifer Hudson), but given how reverential Grande has been to Carey in the past and just how much 'Yes, And?' would play so well into her wheelhouse, the remix ends up being a tad disappointing, sounding thrown together at the last possible moment. Carey, holder of one of the greatest voices ever put to record, sounds like she recorded her lines in a broom cupboard.

If you're looking for a remix of an *Eternal Sunshine* track featuring some '90s legends, I would stick to the *much* better 'The Boy Is Mine' remix with Brandy and Monica!

GEORGE GRIFFITHS

## 'WE CAN'T BE FRIENDS (WAIT FOR YOUR LOVE)'

**Release date:** 8 March 2024
**Written by:** Ariana Grande, Max Martin, Ilya
**Produced by:** Ariana Grande, Max Martin, Ilya

There should be a gold-plated rule in pop music: when in doubt, look to Robyn.

I still can't believe that a song like 'We Can't Be Friends (Wait For Your Love)' exists in Grande's discography, but I'm so happy it does, because it is *so* resonant with the themes of *Eternal Sunshine* and feels so different for her. I called it one of her best songs and I stand by that. Lyrically, melodically and sonically, it's a truly great turnout for her. I never thought she would ever make a song like this, but it makes perfect sense on a record for how adrift the breakdown of a relationship has made you feel. You want to preserve what little of that relationship is left with someone who, for however long, felt like the centre of your world but you find yourself becoming more and more aware of the inescapable truth that too much water has passed under the bridge, that you can *never* go back to the way you were before. There is simply no way that you can be friends and that seems like the most devastating thing in the world. In a way, isn't it?

Much in the way that *Vogue* was clearly a big reference for 'Yes, And?', here 'We Can't Be Friends' takes its cues from perhaps the best breakup song written this century: 'Dancing On My Own' by Robyn.

'Dancing On My Own' was the biggest hit from Robyn's masterpiece, 2010's *Body Talk*, a devastatingly sophisticated and experimental pop record that proved to be an influential touchstone for later artists like Charli xcx and Carly Rae Jepsen. Part of its legend, though, is that it was never really that big a hit. Instead, it *influenced* so many hits after that it can't help but be a Rosetta Stone for the template of an electronic pop ballad in the modern day.

Grande, Martin and Ilya are wise enough not to make 'We Can't Be Friends' an out-and-out tribute to Robyn, but the tendrils that connect the two songs are clearly there for anyone to see. Just like 'Dancing On My Own', 'We Can't Be Friends' production is bursting to the seams with emotion. Grande's world, teetering on the edge, is filled with the rumble of drums, like thunder on the horizon or her heartbeat in her chest. The production is more minimal than you might think, but the track doesn't feel empty. Quite the opposite, in fact.

What Grande is talking about here she's never actually fully opened on. One of the things I like so much about 'We Can't Be Friends' is since there is no definitive answer, you must fill in the gaps yourself. When she pleads on the chorus, is that a direct nod of defeat to her relationship with Dalton Gomez, or do the references to papers and pens instead mean the media? For me, I like to think the answer lies somewhere in-between; that here, she both admits that her marriage with Gomez is broken beyond repair and accepts that she's also caught in a toxic relationship with the press. One day, she's the darling of the moment, the next her personal life is splattered all over the headlines. Being able to accept that she cannot (and will not) control either of these things is what gives her serenity by the song's end. Sometimes, you must just burn the bridge behind you and keep on walking.

Remember when I talked about Michel Gondry's 2004 film, *Eternal Sunshine of the Spotless Mind*, and its influence on the album's title and meaning? Well, Grande takes it one step further on the video for 'We Can't Be Friends (Wait For Your Love)', which is a direct visual remake of the film. Much like in Gondry's film, the video concerns a couple's choice to erase each other's memories following the breakdown of their romance. Whereas, in Gondry's film, we mainly follow Jim Carrey's character Jim, the 'We Can't Be Friends' video is focused on Grande's character, Peaches, who elects to have the memory-erasing procedure at the Brighter Days clinic. Her boyfriend, played in the clip by *American Horror Story* star Evan Peters, is never named.

The conceit of the video is, by Grande's own admission, basically the entire plot of *Eternal Sunshine of the Spotless Mind* condensed into a three-minute music video. Peaches is allowed to walk through her memories with her ex-boyfriend, whose visage slowly disappears (in one scene he's replaced by a dog) as her memories are adapted. When the video closes out, Peaches leaves the clinic and walks past Peters' character, although both seem to have forgotten the other entirely.

I like the video, although it's just a bit too much of a straight homage for my liking. For me, the track really came alive on a live performance on *Saturday Night Live* in 2024. Grande has both hosted and performed at *SNL* many times over the years but I don't think she's ever been better than the night she performed 'We Can't Be Friends (Wait For Your Love)' for the first and so far, only time.

During the performance, Grande is made up as her Peaches character from the music video. She starts the performance watching TV mindlessly before getting to her feet as 3D screens around her turn her room into a churning waterfall and then an open sky. Her vocal performance here is extraordinary and completely enthralling. She sings completely with her chest and you can *feel* every emotion practically dripping from every word.

'We Can't Be Friends (Wait For Your Love)' was released in tandem with the *Eternal Sunshine* album on 8 March 2024 and it was another success straight of the gate for Grande. At the time of writing, it is her ninth and most recent US Number 1 single. She is tied joint-seventh with both Katy Perry and Beyoncé in the list of female artists with the most Billboard Hot 100 Number 1 hits. It was also a great showing for Max Martin; 'We Can't Be Friends' was his twenty-fifth overall US Number 1.

He retains the record as the producer with the most Number 1 hits in America, and as far as songwriters go, 'We Can't Be Friends' saw him overtake John Lennon (!) in the all-time rankings. Only Paul McCartney, with twenty-seven hits, has more.[8]

With all this in mind, it's nice to view 'We Can't Be Friends' as a testament to the continuation and evolution of Grande's long-standing partnership with Martin. How wonderful that such accolades can come from a song this surprising and exciting!

# 9

# Transition into Acting, *Wicked* and Oscar Nomination

To say the live-action adaptation of the musical *Wicked* was a cultural phenomenon is doing it a disservice. In fact, I'd go so far as to say the film was a revelation in many ways, reinvigorating public appetite for musical adaptions following several well-publicised flops (looking at you, *Cats*!) and netting widespread acclaim and Oscar nominations for its two leads, Cynthia Erivo and Ariana Grande.

But let's pull back a bit, first. To understand why *Wicked* was (and still is) such a big deal, we must first look to its origins. The musical *Wicked* first debuted in 2003. It's an adaptation of Gregory Maguire's 1995 bestseller, *Wicked: The Life and Times of the Wicked Witch of the West*, which itself is a quasi-prequel to L. Frank Baum's 1900 novel, *The Wonderful Wizard of Oz*, and its 1939 film adaptation, which memorably starred Judy Garland as Dorothy Gale, a Kansas teenager swept up by a cyclone to the Land of Oz.

In Baum's original text, the Wicked Witch of the West is just one of several obstacles that Dorothy and her companions, the Scarecrow, the Tin Man and the Cowardly Lion, must overcome to help her find her way back home to Kansas. But in the 1939 film, the structure of a Hollywood screenplay mandated the film must have a main villain and so the Wicked Witch of the West underwent a dramatic makeover. Now, she was an evil sorceress supreme, with ivy-green skin, a cackle that could crack glass and a menacing, operatic temper, perfectly played by actress Margaret Hamilton.

Maguire's original *Wicked* novel combines the mythos of both Baum's book and the film. His Wicked Witch (who was unnamed in both 1900 and 1939) is now called Elphaba (pronounced like 'LFB', in tribute to Baum) and the novel charts her attendance to Shiz University, where she meets Galinda Upland (the future Glinda the Good Witch) and becomes involved in a political uprising that changes the trajectory of her life forever.

When *Wicked* debuted on Broadway in 2003, it changed (and made) the careers of its two stars: Idina Menzel as Elphaba and Kristin Chenoweth as Galinda. Galinda later changes her name to Glinda, but I'll call her Galinda throughout just to avoid confusion. Its original Broadway run was highly acclaimed and turned both Menzel and Chenoweth into stars. In 2004, it received ten nominations at the Tony Awards, the biggest night in American theatre, with Menzel eventually scooping Best Actress in a Musical over her co-star Chenoweth, who was also nominated in the same category.

Given its massive successes – *Wicked* is still playing on both Broadway and London's West End, where it initially opened in 2006 – a live-action adaptation of the music was inevitable. Almost from the moment *Wicked* opened, there was talk of an impending feature film or even a TV series being in active development.

The first real, concrete news we got of a *Wicked* adaptation was in 2016, when Universal Pictures announced that a *Wicked* film would arrive in cinemas on 20 December 2019, directed by Stephen Daldry (*Billy Elliot*, *The Hours*).[1] However, the film would suffer the first of what would be many setbacks. In 2018, production (which had still yet to cast its two leads) was paused and *Wicked*'s spot in the release schedule taken up by Universal's other big musical adaptation, *Cats*.

Now, *Cats* is important because it may be one of the worst films I have ever seen in my life, a sentiment echoed by almost every critic and cinemagoer who went to see it. *Cats* was not just a critical failure, but a commercial one too. It made an estimated $75.5 million[2] at the global box office; the budget was purported to be in the range of $80–100 million,[3] meaning the film had failed to recoup its budget during its time in cinemas.

*Cats*' failure came just months before the incoming COVID-19 pandemic shuttered down theatres across the globe for months. At the time, *Wicked* was still set to arrive in cinemas in 2021, but there were further complications incoming. Daldry left the production in 2020, to be replaced the next year by Jon M. Chu, who had recently helmed the well-received *In The Heights* musical adaptation.

With Chu at the helm, though, things started to move more quickly than before. Erivo and Grande were cast as Elphaba and Galinda that same year. The rest of the cast was filled out with *Bridgerton* heart-throb Jonathan Bailey as Fiyero, Ethan Slater as Boq, Michelle Yeoh as Madame Morrible and Jeff Goldblum as the Wizard of Oz.

Ariana had made no secret of the fact that playing Galinda in an adaptation of *Wicked* was a dream role for her. By her own admission, she'd heard whispers of the casting process during the pandemic and set her agents at CAA on the case of securing her an audition, years before the film had even started active production.

'As soon as I caught whispers that [a *Wicked* movie] was going to happen at all,' she recalled to Jimmy Fallon, 'I started to mentally prepare myself and my team. I told them "if this *is* really happening and they're going to start seeing people for it, I want to be so prepared. I want to take all the acting lessons, all the singing lessons. I want to train my voice. I have to honour this the way that [the role] requires."'[4]

On her devotion to securing the role, *Wicked* producer Marc Platt said, 'Ariana Grande more or less stalked me for ten years. In her very sweet way, she'd ask to come see me whenever she heard maybe there was a movie in the works.' One of her first requests upon signing with Hollywood talent agency CAA in 2011, aged eighteen, was that an eventual *Wicked* film be seen as a priority for her career.[5]

Elphaba and Galinda were two of the most sought-after jobs in recent memory. Ariana had to audition five times for the role, with Chu memorably asking her to come in without make-up and the elaborate trappings of her pop-star persona.

'Everything about me,' Grande recalled on *The Zach Sang Show*, 'I had to deconstruct [myself] to prove [to Chu and the studio] that I could handle taking on this other person.'

Competition for the role was wide-ranging; Amanda Seyfried, Reneé Rapp and Dove Cameron all confirmed that they had also auditioned for Galinda, but when push came to shove, Chu could clearly tell that Ariana's take on the character was not the most surprising but the most evocative and exciting, *especially* given her palpable chemistry, on and off screen, with Cynthia Erivo.

'She was so funny,' Chu recalled of Ariana's audition. 'She was so interesting, like she was from another planet. She was going Galinda, but not [impersonating Kristin Chenoweth]. We kept bringing her back, she was always the most interesting person in the room. The only Galinda we wanted to see was her.'[6]

And my, what a revelation Grande is in *Wicked*! Erivo has a *lot* of heavy lilting to do as Elphaba; she is both the emotional and moral centre of the film and it would be easy to write Grande off as a result, given that Galinda is seen as more comic relief than anything. But Ariana does not treat Galinda as a side character, as someone to laugh *at* (like her character, Cat Valentine in *Victorious*, for instance). As a performer, she seemed to inherently understand what makes Galinda such a rich and fascinating character in *Wicked*; that despite her outwardly 'ditzy' appearance, she is a smart, sociopolitically minded and incredibly ambitious woman. Yes, she's privileged. Galinda's family, the Uplands, are wealthy and prestigious enough that she can get engaged to Fiyero Tigelaar, a prince from Winkie Country, something that Elphaba simply couldn't. However, she wants more for herself and is desperate to get it by any means.

Galinda's charm — and my, does she have charm, buckets of it to spare — is therefore more like an armour that she chooses to wear. A weapon that she's honed to intentionally make people underestimate her. Which, of course, everyone but Elphaba does.

Scene for scene, I honestly think Ariana gives the best performance in *Wicked*. She is so charismatic, you're surprised she doesn't just simply leap out of the screen when she's singing 'Popular' or leading the intricate, thrilling full-scale dance number in 'What Is This Feeling?' We all know through their very chaotic and disarmingly emotional press tour that she and Erivo share a rare connection and this is only amplified by their time on screen together. Seeing the full first part of *Wicked*, you really do understand Chu's need to split the film in two. You get *so* much time dedicated in the first half to setting up the friendship between these two women, in a way you just wouldn't if the narrative was squeezed into a two-hour run-time.

By the end of the film, Galinda makes her choice not to follow Elphaba in revolting against the Wizard and Madame Morrible's plan to enslave the talking Animals of Oz as the only logical conclusion her character can draw in the moment. She *wants* to follow Elphaba but knows that she can't. Everything she has strived for – magic, power, status – would be ripped away from her if she did and that just isn't something that is compatible with her view of the world, or how she's been taught to survive in it.

Despite its tortured time in development and numerous setbacks in the creation and filming, *Wicked*'s first part arrived in cinemas worldwide on 22 November 2024. It was rapturously received. During the opening week, the film grossed $112.5 million at the domestic US box office, setting a record for the largest opening of a Broadway adaptation in America (the previous record, *Into The Woods*, debuted with $31.1 million).

Globally, *Wicked* holds the largest-ever first week haul for a Broadway musical adaptation too, with $169.2 million, far outgrossing the previous record-holder, 2012's *Les Misérables*, with $103 million. With a total worldwide gross of $755.8 million, *Wicked* is now the highest-grossing movie musical of all time (the previous record holder was 2008's *Mamma Mia!*). Its commercial success was only further compounded by the film's significant critical acclaim. Both Erivo and Grande received fawning reviews, with Grande's performance notably being hailed as a star-making role and in many critics' eyes the highlight of the film. Of course, in this modern age everything is helped with a viral moment and *Wicked* had *so* many viral moments, mostly thanks to its press tour.

Paired together, Erivo and Grande's hyper-emotional bond was both bizarre and incredibly refreshing to see. No one could doubt that these two women *loved* working together.

'There's a wonderful synergy when you're working with a person who gets it, and they can look in your eyes and know exactly what you need, when you need it, without you having to say it,' Erivo once said of working with Grande. 'To know where we are together allows us to walk into a room hand in hand, and really strongly, it gives us a particular kind of strength that allows us to be one, be really trusting of each other.'[7]

For Grande, her obvious connection with Erivo 'is continuing to grow, and has been growing since day one. We both made the conscious decision when we met to take care of each other, and that's what we have done in the realest of ways, every step. I always say this, but it's one of the things that I think we're most proud of.'[8]

One thing *I* was holding space for, however, was some real recognition of Erivo and Grande's work in the film. Thankfully, I got what I wished for. Rare for a modern-day musical and even rarer still for a full-on fantasy film, *Wicked* became a hot shot awards contender. It was the second-most nominated film of the night at the 97th Academy Awards, tying arthouse historical drama *The Brutalist* with ten nominations apiece. These included nods for Best Picture, Best Director for Jon M. Chu, Best Actress for Erivo and, most thrillingly, Best Supporting Actress for Grande.

Any actor's first Oscar nomination is something to celebrate, but it's even more special when it comes from their official big-screen debut. I would love to say that Ariana was a front-runner to pick up that Academy Award, but it wasn't to be. From the start of the awards season, it was clear that Zoe Saldaña's turn in the musical comedy-drama *Emilia Pérez* was the performance to beat in the Best Supporting Actress category, even though you could well argue Saldaña's character is *the* main focus of the film.

That proved to be true when on the night Saldaña did indeed pick up her first Oscar for her work on *Emilia Pérez*. Erivo also went home empty-handed, losing Best Actress to Mikey Madison for the romantic comedy-drama *Anora*. Still, while winning the Oscar would, of course, have been amazing, I'd argue that the greatest win was this film and these performances getting a look-in at all. Certainly, during recent times, genres like fantasy have struggled to gain a foothold with Oscar voters, so these nominations alone prove not only is this tide slowly shifting, but *Wicked*'s hype-train was simply too big to ignore.

And, of course, if they didn't get them this year, there's always next year!

We'll never know the effect on Grande's career and outlook if *Wicked* had flopped as spectacularly as, say, *Cats*, but we can tell a lot about what's going to happen next for her following its considerable success. Many times, during *Wicked*'s press tour and awards campaign, she stated that she was looking to focus more on acting in this next phase of her career.

As she told the *Variety Awards Circuit Podcast*, acting is her 'focus' right now and although she had planned a smaller-scale tour between the releases of both *Wicked* and *Wicked: For Good*, plans for any kind of live shows have now been scrapped indefinitely.

'I'm really, really grateful to be focused on acting,' she said. 'I feel so at home here. I hope that's okay.'[9]

While another tour may be off the cards, Ariana hasn't fully retired from the pop-star life. As we'll see, the break in promotion between the two *Wicked* films did allow her to dip her toes back into the world of pop music, with material more authentic than ever.

ARIANA GRANDE

## 'WHAT IS THIS FEELING?' with Cynthia Erivo

**Release date:** 22 November 2024
**Written by:** Stephen Schwartz
**Produced by:** Stephen Schwartz, Greg Wells, Stephen Oremus

When we meet them in the 1939 adaptation of *The Wizard of Oz*, the Wicked Witch of the West and Glinda the Good Witch are opposing enemies. One of them is a despot feared throughout the land, looking to avenge the death of her sister, while the other is the seeming champion of the downtrodden, who sets the plot in motion to kill the Wicked Witch when she gifts Dorothy Gale a pair of enchanted shoes that belonged to the Witch's sister, killed by the cyclone that brought Dorothy to Oz.

*Wicked* asks both how they got here and manages to fill in the gaps between the start of *The Wizard of Oz* and the two's first meeting. The conceit of *Wicked* – both the original novel, the Broadway adaptation and its subsequent live-action film – is that Elphaba and Galinda *used* to be friends and it's exactly the fracturing of this friendship that ends up at their iconic meeting, now as rivals and sworn enemies, at the start of *The Wizard of Oz*.

The journey of Elphaba and Galinda's relationship is, more than anything, the backbone to *Wicked*. It gives the story its emotional depth and us the ability to see this timeless fantasy story through a brand-new lens.

'What Is This Feeling?' drops us right into the beginning of them meeting each other, when forced to share a room when they both attend Shiz University. To say that they rub each other up the wrong way would be an understatement.

For my money, 'What Is This Feeling?' is the first truly great song from *Wicked* and the first great set-piece of the movie. It sets the stage extravagantly for what's to come, giving us our first glimpses into the personal and political issues that divide Elphaba and Galinda, and providing hints as to how they will eventually bridge this gap.

The divide is clear from the very start of the song. Galinda, as we've already discussed, comes from a very well-off family and has a loving mother and father who have helped her move into university. For Elphaba, however, her skin colour has made her a pariah, while the death of her mother has complicated her relationship with her father, who depends on Elphaba to care for her disabled sister, Nessarose, the future Wicked Witch of the East.

You can clearly see the battle lines being drawn. Both Elphaba and Galinda are brilliant students, yes, but Elphaba comes to Shiz despite her social standing and home life, whereas Galinda's rise has been perpetrated by them. They don't just come from different worlds, they speak in different languages in the way that they can interact with the world. Galinda expects (and wants) everyone to fall in love with her, while Elphaba cares little for the opinion of others and simply wants to be left alone in peace. Of course, sparks were going to fly between them.

So, yes, the 'feeling' that exists between Elphaba and Galinda on their first meeting is one of indescribable loathing. Not great! But if anything, this barely-hid contempt the two of them instantly share for each other is what makes 'What Is This Feeling?' such a fun number to experience when watching *Wicked*. What they *don't* know, of course, is that they've both misjudged the other – but *Wicked*'s first half is nothing if a comedy of errors, so we must let them work through it.

A stand-out part of 'What Is This Feeling?' is the intricate choreography. Grande leads an entire dance troupe of students in the song's final minutes. It's a dazzling display of form and what I love best about it is that Ariana infuses Galinda with so much joy in this moment. She really is relishing the power of her popularity and what it can do.

*Wicked*'s sound mixer Simon Hayes confirmed to *The Hollywood Reporter* that Erivo and Grande's vocals were mostly recorded live on the set of *Wicked*, at the behest of the two actresses and director Jon M. Chu. Grande herself performed with two mics at all times, one on her right and the other on her left side due to her low-cut dresses.

Erivo, for example, was 'adamant' that she wanted to sing 'Defying Gravity' live. Hayes says that as a result, both actresses were 'given the freedom to express themselves emotionally' while performing. [10]

ARIANA GRANDE

## 'POPULAR'

**Release date:** 22 November 2024
**Written by:** Stephen Schwartz
**Produced by:** Stephen Schwartz, Greg Wells, Stephen Oremus

If there's one thing Galinda Upland cares about, it's stature. We know this almost from the first moment we meet her. She arrives at Shiz University and cares very much what other people think of her. Her outward performance is a spectacle to not just make everyone like her, but to make them in awe of her – she *wants* to dazzle them.

This is one of the main reasons for her disagreements with Elphaba, someone who really doesn't care what other people think of her. But for Galinda, popularity is her way of manoeuvring through the world, of *interacting* with it. So, she just can't understand why Elphaba isn't interested in this and why she doesn't know how much it could help her out. 'Popular', therefore, is Galinda's way of reaching out to Elphaba and welcoming her into her world. Popularity, after all, is power – and there's nothing Galinda Upland craves more.

In the context of *Wicked*'s narrative, 'Popular' takes place after a pivotal event for Elphaba and Galinda. The Winkie (yes, that's a real word) Prince Fiyero has just arrived at Shiz University and entrances both Elphaba and Galinda, who makes it her mission to become Fiyero's girlfriend. Fiyero throws a party at the Ozdust Ballroom and Galinda, still feuding with Elphaba, invites her along as a joke, giving her a pointed hat to wear and complimenting her on it, before Elphaba arrives at the ball, hat and all, and is ridiculed by the student body.

Immediately seeing the error of her ways, Galinda and Elphaba finally call a truce on their feud. 'Popular' is an extension of that, detailing the process in which Galinda instructs Elphaba on how to change her image to improve her social standing at Shiz. Whereas 'What Is This Feeling?' sees Elphaba and Galinda butt heads with their opposing world views, 'Popular' sees them meeting in the middle, albeit somewhat begrudgingly.

Elphaba, at least, is so relieved to have finally found a friend that she's willing to hear Galinda out, to see things from her point of view. She allows Galinda to *try* and change her, although that's not the point of 'Popular'. Elphaba isn't really changed by Galinda's meddling, but instead comes to understand her better and the good heart that exists behind the frivolity. By the end of the songs, there is a fast-growing friendship established between the two – in fact, they're well on their way to becoming sisters.

'Popular' was the first musical number shot for *Wicked* and the first chance for Grande to show everything she could do as Galinda. As such, she throws herself headfirst into a committed performance. The number is filmed on actually quite small sets – from Galinda and Elphaba's shared room and then off into a corridor for a dance break – but Ariana acts as if she's back on stage, in front of a 200,000-strong crowd.

Playing Galinda also required her to 'completely retrain' her style of singing, which was much more operatic than, say, her previous experience of singing pop songs like 'Into You'.

'Galinda exists fully in this *coloratura* soprano register,' she told Jimmy Kimmel. 'I had to train to learn how to sing it and make that part of my voice a lot stronger, to train my vowel sounds and my consonants. I started training three months from my first audition.'[11]

Going even further than this, Grande's own voice coach for *Wicked*, Eric Vetro, revealed that her performance of 'Popular' was captured in one take.

'You always want to approach someone's voice from every possible angle,' Vetro said, remembering the months of intensive training he underwent with Ariana. 'You have to stretch it so it becomes more limber and flexible.'[12]

'Popular' is perhaps the best shot and choreographed number in the whole film. A huge part of this is due to Grande. Dressed in a puffy pink peignoir the colour of cotton candy, she floats, jumps and kicks around the screen, imbuing Galinda with a barely contained glee as she starts to plot Elphaba's makeover. I *love* her performance as Galinda, which is crystallised in its purest form in 'Popular'. I really do think that when she was put forward as an Oscar contender, 'Popular' would have been the part in the film where most people sat back and said, *yes, I get it now.* For *anyone* playing Galinda in *Wicked*, the ghost of Kristin Chenoweth's take on the role looms large (much the same as Idina Menzel does for Elphaba). I can certainly see where Ariana used Chenoweth's take on the role as inspiration – those operatic high notes! – but she creates enough distance between them that she makes the role her own.

Also, may I say how much I appreciate her enunciation of the word 'popular' in the song? Very pleasing to the ears!

Physicality is such an important factor here. Where 'Popular', and Grande, really shine is when the musical number breaks out of the dorm room and into the adjoining corridor. Chu and *Wicked*'s cinematographer, Alice Brooks, give 'Popular' an extended ending – with a dance break! Grande's Galinda really comes alive here; the set is dimmed with pink lights galore, like we've just entered her world. In a way, we have. For these moments, *Wicked* is Ariana's film, and Ariana's film alone. Here, she seems to have been transplanted, for a few minutes, away from the Land of Oz and into a 1950s movie musical with Fred Astaire. She uses her extravagant costume like a prop; she fluffs it out, she throws it every which way, essentially helping to elongate her body and fill the space. Grande even does a high kick! How could you not gag at that? Of course, the song ends on a funny little twist. Yes, Galinda declares, Elphaba *will* be popular . . . but not *quite* so popular as she is.

'Popular' has always been one of the most. . . . well . . .

*popular* songs from *Wicked*, and with Grande attached, its release as a number on the film's official soundtrack was always going to bring some form of commercial success. Of course, the big push from the soundtrack was always going to be 'Defying Gravity' – but 'Popular' didn't do so badly either! It peaked at Number 53 on the Billboard Hot 100 but did a much better job in the UK, reaching Number 13.

Talk about popularity!

GEORGE GRIFFITHS

## 'DEFYING GRAVITY' with Cynthia Erivo

**Release date:** 22 November 2024
**Written by:** Stephen Schwartz
**Produced by:** Stephen Schwartz, Greg Wells, Stephen Oremus

Whenever someone thinks about *Wicked* the musical, they probably think of one thing and one thing only: 'Defying Gravity', the musical's centrepiece and most iconic song.

Notable for Elphaba's battle cry that ends the song. All together now: *woooooahhhh-aaaahhhh-ahhhhhhh!* 'Defying Gravity' is that rare song that seems to have transcended its roots. You wouldn't necessarily have even *seen* the original musical to recognise it, or know it. It was so popular, in fact, that the original Elphaba, Idina Menzel, even released it as a single, although the more 'pop' version she recorded isn't very good.

'Defying Gravity' has a very important function in *Wicked* besides being its best song. It's the moment that brings the musical's first act to a close; where Elphaba, now seeing that the Wizard of Oz has been trying to manipulate her and use her innate magical gifts to help enslave the Animals of Oz, decides that rebellion is the only way forward. This is the moment where Elphaba Thropp *becomes* the Wicked Witch of the West with the twist being, of course, she was never wicked but instead a victim of political propaganda.

Ask anyone who has ever seen *Wicked* on the stage and they will most likely gush about the performance of 'Defying Gravity'. It's the best bit of the entire show; to simulate Elphaba taking flight on an enchanted broomstick, the actress playing Elphaba is launched into the sky on a cherry picker, the machinery covered by material the same colour of the actress's dress, which also gives the further illusion of her flying higher and higher into the sky.

It is, to put it bluntly, *a moment*. But 'Defying Gravity' was always going to be a problem for any *Wicked* adaptation. It is *such* a moment that it entirely kills the forward momentum. You need a fifteen-minute interval just to get over it and reset, which is something that wouldn't be afforded to a standard Hollywood two-hour film. So, it makes total sense that in a two-part *Wicked* adaptation, 'Defying Gravity' is the moment that closes the first film (in fact, I'd even go so far as to say they *had* to split the film in two just to accommodate it).

Grande is not the focus of 'Defying Gravity'. That would be impossible as this is both Erivo and Elphaba's defining moment in the film. However, her presence only adds to the narrative weight. 'Defying Gravity' finds Elphaba and Galinda at a final crossroads. Their image of the Wizard of Oz as a noble, powerful statesman has been shattered. In fact, he lacks power entirely, having arrived in Oz from Earth in a mysterious storm. Now hailed a hero, he's suppressing the Animals of Oz to keep himself in power. He needs Elphaba and her magic to continue to do so, but after seeing the oppression of the Animals first-hand, Elphaba vows to fight him.

Fleeing the Emerald City, she asks Galinda to come with her and help stir a rebellion. But rebellion is not in Galinda Upland's blood. The fact that Galinda refuses to go with Elphaba is, of course, a foregone conclusion, but it's a compliment to both Grande and Erivo's performances how *real* this moment – and how potent the devastation over their parting – feels here. Most of this is thanks to an extended run-time for *Wicked*. Now no longer concerned with wrapping up the entire musical's narrative in one go, it can devote a lot more time to Elphaba and Galinda's relationship. As I've said, it really is the heart and the soul of the film, its backbone. 'Defying Gravity' continues this focus. The song is not sung entirely in one go as it is on stage. Instead, Chu and screenwriters Winnie Holzman and Dana Fox split up the song with several interludes, mostly focused on Elphana and Galinda's escape from the Wizard's palace, setting the stage for their eventual parting.

Giving 'Defying Gravity' this breathing space – and really making you work to get all the way to the end – is, I think, a genius decision and one of the most interesting flourishes that's emerged from *Wicked*'s adaptation to the screen. While, yes, this is entirely Erivo's moment, you can't reach its bravura climax without Grande's contributions. Her performance is full of yearning here, stripped away from the egregious showmanship she'd so readily displayed in 'What Is This Feeling?' or 'Popular'.

Coming in right at the end of the film, where Galinda makes her decision to stay with the Wizard, she proves she can act dramatically as well as comedically. You see the visage behind Galinda's persona crack, if only for a moment.

As the most recognisable song from *Wicked*, you will not be surprised when I tell you Erivo and Grande's rendition of the track was the most successful release from the film's soundtrack. It was the highest-charting song from *Wicked* in the US, peaking at Number 44 on the Billboard Hot 100, while *Wicked* mania clearly reached fever pitch in the UK. 'Defying Gravity' peaked at Number 7 on the Official Singles Chart. It was Grande's twenty-third (!) UK Top 10 hit and the first ever for Cynthia Erivo.

The entire thing came full circle at the start of 2025, when Erivo and Grande performed a mash-up of *The Wizard of Oz*-inspired tracks at the Oscars; Grande took 'Over The Rainbow', while Erivo sang 'Home' from *The Wiz* before they joined forces for 'Defying Gravity'. We even get an adapted cherry-picker stunt for the end of the song, with Grande graciously waiting on the side of the stage, cheering on, as Erivo hits that high note, that battle cry to the oppressed and forgotten.

The only question remaining is, how on earth do they top this?

# 10

# *Eternal Sunshine Deluxe: Brighter Days Ahead, Wicked: For Good* and What's Next?

So, what's next for Ariana Grande?

There's still one *Wicked* movie left to release, she's slowly but surely becoming attached to new films in development post-Oscar buzz and, if the acting jobs dry up, I'm sure Max Martin will be ready and waiting for her in the studio.

When *Wicked: For Good* is released in November 2025, Ariana will find herself at a most interesting crossroads. The first *Wicked* film legitimised her acting career in the grandest way possible and she would be a fool not to capitalise on this and strike while the iron's hot, just as she did with her early albums. Scoring an Oscar nomination for your first film role is the kind of pedigree most actors can only aspire to and you get the sense that, right now, Hollywood is Grande's oyster. She almost certainly has her pick of parts.

One thing that *Wicked* proved is that she's a comedic

actress of rare ability. The recent news that she'll be joining the cast for the fourth *Meet The Parents* film, *Fockers In-Law* with Ben Stiller and Robert De Niro[1], shows that she's playing to her strengths for now, although it will be important for her career longevity to branch out at some point.

Of course, Grande's music career is arguably in the healthiest state it's ever been. *Eternal Sunshine* not only showed her growth as a songwriter and a producer, but its two back-to-back Number 1 singles also proved she was still an active hitmaker. She also proved that she was still entuned to the pulse of popular music, becoming the biggest A-list act to feature on the remixed version of British pop star Charli xcx's acclaimed 2024 album, *Brat*.

*Brat* is an extraordinary record and a landmark moment for Charli, an artist who, for most of her career, was a perennial underdog. A pop star who was *just* too ahead of the curve. *Brat* was the moment when Charli finally allowed the mainstream to catch up with her and she milked that moment for all it was worth.

On the original LP, 'Sympathy Is A Knife' is one of *Brat*'s most striking tracks. An anthem about a very specific kind of envy you feel when someone you deem to be more 'successful' than you enters your social circle. It's wildly contested to be written about Taylor Swift, the biggest pop star of this generation, and her short-lived fling with The 1975 frontman, Matty Healy. Charli herself is engaged to The 1975 drummer and Healy's creative partner, George Daniel.

For *Brat*'s remix album, *Brat And It's Completely Different But Also Still Brat*, 'Sympathy Is A Knife's titular knife is not a metaphor for jealousy, but the intrusion of the press. Grande really goes there, criticising the press's obsession with her body.

The song's focus shifts from the personal to the societal. What, it seems to ask, does being in the public eye ask of those with fame? Why is it OK for female artists to constantly fend off this scrutiny and character assassination when the same is never asked of their male counterparts? How long, they ask, would *you* be willing to cope with this constant pressure, this constant pain?

'Sympathy Is A Knife' was invigorating, but proved not to be the final release from Grande before *Wicked: For Good* hits cinemas in November 2025. If there's one thing that a major album by an A-list pop act must have in 2025, it's an expanded deluxe edition. These are becoming *de rigueur* again, a handy trick to help elongate a star's album campaign while they either tour or, in Grande's case, are too busy with other commitments to launch into a brand-new era.

The optimum deluxe edition release must act as an expansion and a continuation of the ideas and themes of the records it follows on from. This is exactly what we find on *Eternal Sunshine Deluxe: Brighter Days Ahead*, a sparse but concise sequel to *Eternal Sunshine* that near enough picks up from where we left off. It's self-analytical in the way all the best tracks from *Eternal*

*Sunshine* were, yes, but now there's an added layer of melancholy too.

*Brighter Days Ahead* contains some of the most emotionally complex and thematically resonant material of Ariana Grande's career thus far. Over just six tracks, she manages to say *a lot*: about the ramifications of her divorce, her new relationship with Ethan Slater and how she now finds herself mourning for the past in the present. *Eternal Sunshine*'s own name reflects the urge to forget all the things that hurt us, so that we can move on. But on *Brighter Days Ahead*, she seems to accept that you can never totally forget about the pain because it's what moulds you. It's what keeps you going, determined to find those brighter days ahead.

*Brighter Days Ahead* acts as a coda to this act of Grande's career. We don't quite know when she will return, but if this is how she signs off now, I think it's a pretty good way to go. It functions so well because it doesn't sound like a direct continuation of the soundscape of *Eternal Sunshine*. This is a collection of songs that are much more melancholic and reflective. In less sure hands, it could have resulted in the barometer plummeting all the way towards 'depressing' but its most obvious references – Robyn, Lana Del Rey – save it from being totally morose. Because this is not an obituary for Grande's lost love, rather it's an epilogue: the end of one story, ready for a fresh one to start.

Given the tight schedule between the two *Wicked* films, it was never guaranteed (or expected) that Ariana would put as much promotion into *Brighter Days Ahead* as she had in the past with projects like *My Everything*, but the release of this deluxe edition was compounded by one of the most experimental and ambitious undertakings of her career thus far – her very own short film!

Pop music has been obsessed with visual concept albums for a long while now. Beyoncé, Queen of All, has released the only two that are worth bothering with: 2013's *Beyoncé* and 2016's *Lemonade*. They are a *very* hard trick to pull off. For every one that succeeded on a thematic level, like Halsey's accompanying film to her 2021 masterpiece *If I Can't Have Love, I Want Power*, you get something like Jennifer Lopez's 2024 disaster, *This Is Me . . . Now: A Love Story*, a lesson in hubris to the tune of $20 million of Lopez's own money and the definitive proof that her days as a pop star had come to a crashing halt.

Grande's attempt – the short film *Brighter Days Ahead* – doesn't reach the heights of *Lemonade*, but is by no means a disaster. Directed once again by Christian Breslauer, the film itself is a direct sequel to 'We Can't Be Friends (Wait For Your Love)', where we catch up with its protagonist, Peaches, now an old woman, who pays one last visit to the Brighter Days Ahead clinic to revisit some memories from her past. But Ariana constantly blurs the lines between fact and fiction here. When Peaches watches her parents' wedding video, it's that of Ariana's own parents, Joan and Edward.

More moving still is that the home video features Ariana's maternal grandparents, Frank Grande Sr and Marjorie 'Nonna' Grande. Sadly, this would be Ariana's beloved grandmother's final appearance in her music. The Grande family announced in a joint statement that Nonna had died on 17 June 2025, aged ninety-nine, surrounded by her family.

'Marjorie (Nonna) Grande passed peacefully in her home and was surrounded by her family and loved ones for every moment of her last few weeks,' the statement read. 'We thank you for your love, support and for respecting our privacy as we grieve and celebrate her beautiful, extraordinary life.'[2]

Despite being in her late-eighties when her granddaughter shot to superstardom, Nonna became a beloved figure for Ariana's fans. The singer herself clearly adored her grandmother, lovingly riffing her *Sopranos*-esque Italian-American drawl in many public appearances.

Nonna was also present in some of Ariana's music. She supplied spoken-word interludes to two songs, 'Bloodline' from *Thank U, Next* and 'Ordinary Things' from *Eternal Sunshine*. When 'Ordinary Things' debuted on the Billboard Hot 100 at Number 58 following the album's release, Nonna became the oldest act ever to earn a charting single in the US.

Nonna's last public appearance before her death was via a video message sent to Ariana when the singer was promoting *Wicked* on *The Drew Barrymore Show*.

'I am so proud of you,' she says in the video. 'You

make me so proud. Your talent is marvellous. I love you with all my heart.'³

While the songs on *Brighter Days Ahead* are undeniably brilliant – a victory lap for Grande, essentially – they weren't a massive commercial success. Upon release, none of the re-release cuts debuted inside the US Top 10 ('Twilight Zone' got closest – peaking at Number 18), while only one song entered the UK Top 10 ('Twilight Zone' again, hitting Number 5). *Brighter Days Ahead*, though, did give its parent album enough of a boost to return to Number 1 on the Billboard 200.

Next up for Grande, of course, is *Wicked: For Good*, although the sequel now has the unenviable task of having to prove whether the success bestowed on the original film was a fluke, or this two-part adaptation can be fully pulled off. For my money, I think Ariana will be brilliant and for those asking how they could possibly top 'Popular' or 'Defying Gravity', I think the moment she and Erivo meet back on-screen to perform 'For Good' will be one fans cherish.

Who knows, she might have that second Oscar nomination in the bag!

Whatever Ariana decides to do next – more movies, less music, perhaps investing all her savings into an *r.e.m beauty* artisanal soaps range – the Ariana Grande we're leaving in 2025 is very different to the one I first introduced you to in 2008. Yes, she's conquered the charts across the world, scored numerous streaming records and become one of the most dominant female stars of this pop era, but there's much more to her than that. She's proved that hard work, talent and dedication can take you far. She's never rested on her laurels; she's always moved on to the next thing and has always endeavoured to improve her craft. To see her grow not only as a vocalist, but as a performer, a songwriter and now a producer too, is proof that women in pop music can smash the glass boxes that are placed over them so early in their careers.

Then, of course, there is the music. From *Yours Truly* to *Eternal Sunshine*, era by era and song by song, we've seen Ariana mutate and morph into an artist who is purely, singularly herself. Her best songs are achingly personal, forged in the fires of horror and grief and disaster, but possessing an ebullient core. The central thesis to her work – even when dealing with the death of a loved one, or the ending of a pivotal relationship – is that the dark days will *always* come to an end and brighter ones will *always* be ahead.

GEORGE GRIFFITHS

## 'TWILIGHT ZONE'

**Release date:** 28 March 2025
**Written by:** Ariana Grande, Max Martin, Ilya
**Produced by:** Ariana Grande, Max Martin, Ilya

Sometimes, a breakup can be so intense, so world-ending, that when it's finally over and the dust clears, it all feels like just a dream. On 'Twilight Zone', the emotional heart and foundational track on *Eternal Sunshine Deluxe: Brighter Days Ahead*, Ariana muses on her divorce from Dalton Gomez, the pain of which still leaves scars lingering on her skin, although they are slowly starting to disappear now.

On *Sweetener*, Ariana's healing was akin to learning to love herself again and trying to remain positive, and to keep living in the light. On *Thank U, Next*, we see the after-effects of this – a tremor of chaos that reverberates through the entire LP, supercharged by lust, grief and champagne. But now, Grande is older, and she is wiser. This is not the first world-ending event she's had to experience and she knows what to do now, how to ensure she survives this heartbreak. But that doesn't stop her wondering about the past. Or the future. Any of the little things that you contemplate after a breakup: if you had acted differently, if you said something else, would everything work out? Was it *always* destined to fail?

More than that, 'Twilight Zone' deals directly with

the question that the title of *Eternal Sunshine* asks: is it worth forgetting that this ever happened to you?

Taking its name from the popular American supernatural anthology TV series first broadcast in 1959, 'Twilight Zone' finds Grande coming to amid the ruins of her marriage when she's already started a brand-new relationship. As she surveys the damage, she's fully aware that she has a new life now. A much happier one. So much happier, in fact, that it's making her question the validity of her past. Sometimes, she just can't believe all that happened to her.

The song begins with the chimes of bells. Grande, Max Martin and Ilya bring us in with an almost celestial aura, before a strum of synths plonk us back down to earth. As Grande says, we *are* in the twilight zone, a mirage, a mystery, broadcast in black and white. But the scene she's playing is confusing her, enraging her even. Her ex-partner is such a good actor he should have won as Oscar (considering the timing of which this song was released . . . very prescient, which only adds to the intensity of the burn). Grande's heard he's out and seeing someone new now. Would he like her to call this new woman and tell her what she's *really* getting herself into?

Then comes the second verse, where she spirals her thoughts back to herself. Even now, she says, she's protecting this guy. The songs she's written are all obviously about him, but she's never said anything for or against that. This, at least, is true. Grande has never made a definitive statement either way on her divorce from Dalton

Gomez and never actually ever dissected what the songs on *Eternal Sunshine* mean regarding her relationship with both Gomez and Ethan Slater. 'Twilight Zone', then, just muddies these waters. Once again, we see her using her lyricism to work out her feelings in real time.

The highlight of the song, though, is its chorus. Much like most of *Eternal Sunshine*, the lyrics of 'Twilight Zone' are all Grande's (she is the only credited lyricist on every song on *Brighter Days Ahead*) and defy the sort of 'melodic math' that defined so much of her earlier work with Max Martin. But that chorus? It sounds *so* Swedish. The harmonies and melodies are so concise and tight, and they work in perfect harmony with the lyrics and the meaning they're trying to convey. The synths pop up among the drums as Grande must remind herself of several things: that she's *not* still in love with her ex, she *won't* call him, and she *doesn't* miss him . . .

. . . does she?

I think my favourite thing about 'Twilight Zone' is that we don't know if that's true or not. In one sense, you can take it as Grande affirming this, that she has truly moved on and the only thing confusing her right now is that this past life had ever happened. Or you can read it as she's trying to fool herself into forgetting the past – this is a lie that she's telling herself to keep going. I think that's part of the charm of the song; it could be a celebration of release, it could be a testament to never really knowing when something is over.

Grande has explored the cyclical nature of relationships

ending before, of course, but there's a maturity to her words on 'Twilight Zone' that I find really appealing. This is not the same woman who tried to distract herself through her grief as she had on *Thank U, Next*. On that record, you could tell that her demons, her sadness, were always just rearing up behind her shoulder, just out of shot. Ready to pounce.

Now, it's not that Grande has totally made peace with everything she's experienced, but now she herself is experienced enough to realise that it will not break her. She can keep going. What 'Twilight Zone' does tell us, however, is that even our strongest soldiers have their moments of doubt but it's rising from those doubts where we find our strength to march on.

GEORGE GRIFFITHS

## 'HAMPSTEAD'

**Release date:** 28 March 2025
**Written by:** Ariana Grande, Max Martin, Ilya
**Produced by:** Ariana Grande, Max Martin, Ilya

After the torrent of *Thank U, Next*, Ariana Grande has studiously avoided making any kind of public statement on her personal relationships. In fact, even her divorce from Dalton Gomez, which was made official in March 2024, did not come with an announcement from the star, but the filing of the couple's legal paperwork.[4]

Her relationship with Ethan Slater might now be public knowledge, but there has never been an official confirmation from Grande herself. Well, that's until the track 'Hampstead' was included on *Brighter Days Ahead*. As it stands, this is the most public statement she has made on her relationship with Slater. It might be the only one she ever makes.

If the title doesn't make it obvious, the song relates to Grande's time living in the London borough of Hampstead during the two-year filming of *Wicked*. Many of the revelations about her divorce and the beginnings of her relationship with Slater are dressed up in metaphor or only slyly alluded to on most of *Eternal Sunshine*, but here, she really does commit to the bit. 'Hampstead' is, at its core, a confessional ballad – oh boy, does she confess!

Ariana admits that the start of her relationship with Slater was contentious, yes, with both going through the breakups of long-term relationships at the time. She says, though, that she may have damaged her reputation by getting together with him so soon after his own divorce but in doing so, they both saved themselves from further heartache.

'Hampstead' is cleverer than it seems at first, though. Grande's pen constantly swaps its point of view when you are least expecting it. She talks about her own personal experiences and thoughts in the first verse, but then suddenly in the post-chorus, she directly addresses the media looking in on her and Slater. She's tried (and failed) to live her life in the centre of the media circus. You could read her relationship with Pete Davidson, for example, as an experiment to try and control the media narrative in real time, showing up in each other's social media so often. Clearly, however, that failed. So instead, she's trying the next best thing – just forgetting that the media, the paparazzi and everyone else around her exists.

No one, she says on the track, can know what book she's writing, what move she's going to make next. She's not going to invite the media in to make a spectacle of her life anymore – because look where that got her. Nowhere. Then, on the chorus, we get an injection of haunting melancholia. Here, she admits that she knows the situation she's getting into doesn't seem the most stable. But, she tells us, her voice almost breaking with tension, wouldn't *you* do everything it takes to feel something, anything again?

On 'Hampstead', Ariana doesn't want to be seen by

anyone's point of view but her own. She's tired of people making assumptions about her, constructing narratives around her. She's not going to live or die by *anyone's* opinion now. As the final track on *Brighter Days Ahead* and thus probably the last original Ariana Grande song we are going to hear for some time, where does that leave us, and her?

*Brighter Days Ahead* is a coda to Ariana Grande's time as a pop star. That doesn't mean she'll never make pop music again (she will, she *has* to!) but the next time she emerges from her cocoon, she'll be a different type of pop star entirely. You can already see this evolution taking place on *Brighter Days Ahead*, which wasn't released with a lead single as such and didn't receive any significant promotion beyond its own short film. That helped frame the work as part of one cohesive whole, with no bearing on a Number 1 hit single to tie the campaign together and make it sing.

I think that's what Grande will be looking to do with her material moving forward. She doesn't *need* another Number 1 single – she has more than enough and will be famous until the day she dies. Probably far beyond that. With everything she's learnt in terms of songwriting and production, I think we're starting to see her evolve into a true albums' artist. The type of star who can drop an acclaimed project every two to five years, tour that record and maybe win a Grammy or two but doesn't exist at the centre of the mainstream pop conversation anymore.

That feels good. That feels right. Grande has already had an enviable run as a chart-focused pop star. More than a decade of churning out hits when even her most successful peers, like Taylor Swift or Miley Cyrus, have hit significant fallow periods in-between their successes. Plus, no one can – or should – play the pop game forever. Sometimes, it's good to know when to get out. This doesn't feel like Ariana admitting defeat, it feels like her knowing that – for now – she's taking a well-earned break.

With all the praise and accolades garnered with her role in *Wicked*, how could she not explore acting further? Even her peers in the industry are starting to stand up and take notice of her talent as an actress.

Paul Mescal, the acclaimed Irish actor who has starred in *Normal People* and *All Of Us Strangers*, praised Grande for being 'one of the most talented people on the planet' during their conversation for *Variety*'s 'Actors on Actors' series.

'I think you are brilliant in [*Wicked*],' Mescal told her. 'I just think you're brilliant.'[5]

Oscar winner Ariana DeBose also gushed over Grande's star-making role as Galinda, saying that as a musical comedian, her fellow actress was 'spectacular' and that she was now 'desperate' to work with her'.[6]

DeBose might have to wait for a while, though. Grande's first post-*Wicked* acting role in *Fockers In-Law* has already been set in stone. Other projects, too, are in the works, with *The Hollywood Reporter* speculating that

Ariana had been approached to star in a murder-mystery based on the *Real Housewives* reality series produced by Jennifer Lawrence, as well as a sequel to absurdist 1980s sci-fi comedy *Spaceballs*, although for now as we go to press, her only confirmed next project is *Fockers In-Law*.[7]

'I would love to exist in this space [acting] for a while longer,' Ariana told *Screen Daily* in terms of her future plans. 'I love finding characters that make people feel seen and human. I'd love to continue on this road.'[8]

The Ariana Grande we're saying goodbye to now doesn't seem hardened or embittered by her experiences, even though absolutely no one would blame her if she was. Instead, like 'Hampstead' seems to imply, she's come through on the other side with a great knowledge of who she is, what she wants and what she's capable of. That worth comes from inside herself and doesn't need to be defined by any external factors whatsoever.

We leave her forever changed, altered in ways beyond many people's comprehension, but still, undeniably, herself. Always.

# Acknowledgements

First and biggest thanks go to my editor, Katie Ogunsakin. I can't believe that a decade of sisterhood has culminated in a book deal about Ariana Grande, but was it ever meant to go any other way? Thank you for your unconditional love and support, not just as an editor, but as a friend. You are officially the best hag to ever exist, I love you.

Thank you also to the team at Orion and Seven Dials who pushed this to the finish line: Sarah Fortune, Jane Donovan and Beth Eynon and everyone in their respective teams.

To my wonderful, amazing agent Clare Wallace and everyone at Darley Anderson Children's Agency, thank you for taking a punt on a (very green) wannabe writer three years ago, and sticking by me ever since. I feel so lucky to be surrounded by a team of people who fully understand my vision and my hopes for my career. Thank you for always backing me and advocating for me. We did it kids! Onto the next!

My friends are my lifeblood and my support system. The most important relationship in my life. Thank you for picking me up when I'm down, seeing me through a very tumultuous year and always accompanying me to the Two Brewers when needed. You all know who you are. My best friends. My brothers. My sisters. My stunners. My wives. Even a few husbands. I love you all so very, very much.

I know everyone says this, but I genuinely have the best family in the world. I grew up in a very small village called Gilfach Goch in the Rhondda Valleys in South Wales, not the kind of place where someone grows up wanting to be a writer. To my Mam and Dad, thank you for always believing in me and my dreams and helping me get here. To my brother, Harry, I think you knew this was going to happen even before I did. Love you, bro. To all my other family; my Grancha, Catherine, Robert, Alfie, Hattie . . . love you.

To my Nanny Grancha and Nanny Linda. You are the two most important people to have ever existed. I love you beyond words and explanation. Everything I do, I do to make you proud of me.

And, finally, to Ariana Grande. My good sis! I have never met you, and after this I probably never will, but thank you for being such an amazing pop star. I hope this book helps people understand just a small part of your genius. Pop music is my favourite thing in the world, and I feel honoured to have gotten the chance to write about you. 'Into You' remains the best pop song to ever exist. You really did that.

# Image Credits

p. 1, p. 2 Above, p. 2 Below, p. 3 Above, p. 3 Below, p. 4 Below – Getty Images

p. 4 Above, p. 5 Above, p. 5 Below, pp. 6–7, p. 8 Above, p. 8 Below – Alamy

# Notes

### 1. Career Beginnings and *Victorious*

1 https://www.billboard.com/music/music-news/ariana-grande-billboard-cover-story-dangerous-woman-avoiding-drama-feminism-7377472/
2 https://www.rollingstone.com/music/music-news/how-ariana-grande-and-max-martin-made-problem-the-song-of-the-summer-85685/

### 2. *Yours Truly* and the Beginnings of a Pop Career

1 https://www.billboard.com/music/music-news/mariah-carey-reacts-ariana-grande-queen-of-my-life-1235794393/
2 https://youknowigotsoul.com/interview-harmony-samuels-talks-signature-sound-new-jordin-sparks-album-ariana-grande
3 https://pitchfork.com/reviews/albums/18591-ariana-grande-yours-truly/
4 https://youknowigotsoul.com/interview-harmony-samuels-talks-signature-sound-new-jordin-sparks-album-ariana-grande
5 https://www.billboard.com/music/music-news/ariana-grande-talks-breakout-hit-the-way-watch-new-music-video-1554921/
6 https://www.billboard.com/music/music-news/happening-now-big-things-ahead-for-nickelodeon-star-ariana-grande-1556439/
7 https://www.harpersbazaar.com/celebrity/latest/a43428767/ariana-grande-remembers-ex-mac-miller-10-anniversary-song-the-way/

8. https://www.complex.com/music/a/joe-la-puma/ariana-grande-interview-shadow-of-a-doubt-2013-cover-story
9. https://web.archive.org/web/20131103093452/http://www.mtv.com/news/articles/1711378/ariana-grande-big-sean-the-way-sequel.jhtml
10. http://www.telegraph.co.uk/culture/music/music-news/11158600/Ariana-Grande-relationship-Big-Sean.html

## 3. *My Everything* and the Journey to 'It Girl' Status

1. https://web.archive.org/web/20180407120351/https://www.rollingstone.com/music/news/q-a-ariana-grande-on-yours-truly-and-judging-miley-cyrus-20130911
2. www.rollingstone.com/music/music-news/how-ariana-grande-and-max-martin-made-problem-the-song-of-the-summer-85685/
3. https://www.rollingstone.com/music/music-news/how-ariana-grande-and-max-martin-made-problem-the-song-of-the-summer-85685/
4. https://www.youtube.com/watch?v=ws4EPVrrfqg&t=1237s
5. www.rollingstone.com/music/music-news/how-ariana-grande-and-max-martin-made-problem-the-song-of-the-summer-8568
6. www.mtv.com/news/1820830/iggy-azalea-ariana-grande-problem/
7. https://www.billboard.com/music/music-news/ariana-grande-talks-problem-single-second-album-due-out-6070079/
8. https://z1073.com/austin-mahone-passed-on-ariana-grande-break-free/
9. https://gayety.com/zedd-says-pop-princess-ariana-grande-has-always-been-the-queen-following-wicked-success-shes-never-not-had-a-moment
10. https://www.youtube.com/watch?v=IPAke2nPKDU
11. www.billboard.com/photos/7438089/-billboard-hitmakers-roundtable-photos

12 https://www.billboard.com/music/music-news/miley-cyrus-interview-lost-everything-bangerz-controversy-1235995584/
13 http://hitsdailydouble.com/news&id=272599
14 https://www.youtube.com/watch?v=ws4EPVrrfqg
15 https://www.billboard.com/music/music-news/ariana-grande-billboard-cover-story-dangerous-woman-avoiding-drama-feminism-7377472/
16 https://www.youtube.com/watch?v=IPAke2nPKDU
17 https://www.billboard.com/music/music-news/ariana-grande-original-santa-tell-me-music-video-scrapped-1235601013/
18 https://open.spotify.com/playlist/04b2Ijmol8HH5n56hAakSo

## 4. *Dangerous Woman* – A Career-shifting Statement

1 https://www.billboard.com/music/music-news/ariana-grande-billboard-cover-story-dangerous-woman-avoiding-drama-feminism-7377472/
2 https://www.billboard.com/music/music-news/ariana-grande-billboard-cover-story-dangerous-woman-avoiding-drama-feminism-7377472/
3 https://www.billboard.com/music/music-news/ariana-grande-album-name-dangerous-woman-moonlight-6897341/
4 https://www.youtube.com/watch?v=5-FvFZ0jn9Q
5 https://graziadaily.co.uk/celebrity/news/ariana-grande-interview-feminist-grazia/
6 https://www.digitalspy.com/music/a811029/the-surprising-stories-behind-six-of-ariana-grandes-biggest-hits/
7 https://x.com/PopCrave/status/730077553755598848
8 https://www.riaa.com/gold-platinum/?tab_active=default-award&se=Ariana+Grande
9 http://pitchfork.com/features/lists-and-guides/9981-the-100-best-songs-of-2016/?page=10

10 https://www.instagram.com/p/CO3MO-QpHlKZ/?hl=en&img_index=2
11 https://www.vogue.com/article/ariana-grande-cover-august-2019
12 http://www.instyle.com/fashion/ariana-grande-dangerous-woman-tour-looks

## 5. The Manchester Bombing and *Sweetener*

1 https://www.independent.co.uk/arts-entertainment/music/manchester-attack-read-ariana-grandes-full-statement-benefit-concert-a7758621.html
2 https://www.independent.co.uk/arts-entertainment/music/news/ariana-grande-twitter-manchester-victims-funerals-pay-response-terror-attack-explosion-a7753301.html
3 https://www.thesun.co.uk/news/3720576/ariana-grande-manchester-one-love-gig-london-terror-attack/
4 https://news.sky.com/story/ariana-grande-politely-turns-down-damehood-11594819
5 https://pagesix.com/2018/05/22/mac-millers-blood-alcohol-content-almost-twice-legal-limit-in-dui-crash/
6 https://www.wmagazine.com/story/ariana-grande-mac-miller-twitter-clapback
7 https://www.bbc.co.uk/news/newsbeat-44558078
8 https://www.billboard.com/articles/columns/chart-beat/8472196/ariana-grande-sweetener-number-one-billboard-200-chart
9 https://www.billboard.com/music/pop/ariana-grande-sweetener-producer-savan-kotecha-interview-8472238/
10 https://www.youtube.com/watch?v=FXIeWKGGOrY&t=292s
11 https://www.youtube.com/watch?v=3Fs7XyFcuZE
12 https://www.vogue.co.uk/article/ariana-grande-british-vogue-interview

13  https://www.hollywoodreporter.com/movies/movie-news/ariana-grande-wicked-hit-songs-awards-chatter-podcast-1236126039/

## 6. *Thank U, Next* and the Magic of the Imperial Phase

1  https://www.popjustice.com/briefing/which-artist-will-get-everything-right-in-2015/
2  https://www.bbc.co.uk/news/entertainment-arts-45529229
3  https://pitchfork.com/news/ariana-grande-shares-statement-on-toxic-relationship-with-mac-miller/
4  https://www.vogue.com/article/ariana-grande-cover-august-2019
5  https://www.hollywoodreporter.com/movies/movie-news/ariana-grande-wicked-hit-songs-awards-chatter-podcast-1236126039/
6  https://people.com/music/ariana-grande-calls-pete-davidson-an-amazing-distraction/
7  https://people.com/music/ariana-grande-pete-davidson-split/
8  https://people.com/music/pete-davidson-knew-ariana-grande-engagement-over-after-mac-miller-death/
9  https://people.com/ariana-grande-ptsd-grief-depression-anxiety-sweetener-thank-u-next-8785842
10 https://www.harpersbazaar.com/celebrity/latest/a30678280/billie-eilish-grammy-win-ariana-grande-reaction/
11 https://www.vogue.com/article/ariana-grande-cover-august-2019
12 https://x.com/justinbieber/status/1060573628675219456
13 https://www.billboard.com/music/pop/ariana-grande-billie-eilish-switch-lives-voice-8544990/
14 https://www.yahoo.com/entertainment/lana-del-rey-fangirl-moment-212550048.html
15 https://www.billboard.com/music/awards/ariana-grande-cover-story-billboard-women-in-music-2018-8487877/

16 https://www.nytimes.com/2019/03/19/business/media/ariana-grande-7-rings-rodgers-hammerstein.html
17 https://www.officialcharts.com/chart-news/ariana-grande-s-7-rings-debuts-at-number-1-on-the-official-singles-chart-with-record-breaking-streams__25410/

## 7. *Positions*, Marriage and 'Rain On Me'

1 https://www.vogue.com/article/ariana-grande-cover-august-2019
2 https://music.apple.com/us/playlist/lady-gaga-the-chromatica-interview/pl.8a0d43ae41f14c1d88367fcc9b34b7ec
3 https://www.tiktok.com/@velvetfever/video/7478847926492564758
4 https://www.youtube.com/watch?v=Con_aqCcTVk
5 https://www.youtube.com/watch?v=FX1eWKGGOrY
6 https://www.youtube.com/watch?v=Con_aqCcTVk
7 https://podcasts.apple.com/gb/podcast/ive-been-through-w-ariana-grande/id1092361338?i=1000675893549

## 8. Slowing Down, Divorce and *Eternal Sunshine*

1 https://www.billboard.com/music/music-news/ariana-grande-billboard-cover-story-dangerous-woman-avoiding-drama-feminism-7377472/
2 https://www.poetryfoundation.org/poems/44892/eloisa-to-abelard
3 https://www.billboard.com/music/pop/the-weeknd-praises-ariana-grande-production-skills-beast-pro-tools-1235065529/
4 https://www.thecut.com/article/lilly-jay-divorce-essay-therapy.html
5 https://www.dailymail.co.uk/tvshowbiz/article-13499739/Ariana-Grande-brother-Frankie-gushes-singer-wonderful-boyfriend-Ethan-Slater.html

6   https://www.youtube.com/watch?v=MdLcP8dJls4
7   https://www.bbc.co.uk/news/entertainment-arts-65248558
8   https://www.billboard.com/lists/ariana-grande-we-cant-be-friends-hot-100-number-one-debut/

## 9. Transition into Acting, *Wicked* and Oscar Nomination

1   http://www.hollywoodreporter.com/news/universals-wicked-movie-adaptation-gets-903598/
2   https://www.the-numbers.com/movie/Cats-(2019)
3   https://www.hollywoodreporter.com/news/stars-wars-rise-skywalker-friday-box-office-hits-90m-cats-declawed-1264679
4   https://www.youtube.com/watch?v=z2x4zyxAHfY&t=301s
5   https://www.hollywoodreporter.com/movies/movie-features/ariana-grande-wicked-oscars-music-love-1236132418/
6   https://www.hollywoodreporter.com/video/jon-m-chu-creating-wicked-casting-ariana-grande-as-glinda/
7   https://people.com/cynthia-erivo-says-working-with-ariana-grande-on-wicked-is-a-little-bit-addictive-11714154
8   https://deadline.com/feature/wicked-part-1-cynthia-erivo-ariana-grande-interview-1236171811/
9   https://variety.com/2025/film/awards/ariana-grande-wicked-2-original-song-eternal-sunshine-deluxe-release-1236271770/
10  https://www.hollywoodreporter.com/movies/movie-features/ariana-grande-cynthia-erivo-live-singing-wicked-1236106791/
11  https://www.youtube.com/watch?v=6NNGbkwJJ8I
12  https://www.youtube.com/watch?v=TrAwhy5AbAo&t=357s

## 10. *Eternal Sunshine Deluxe: Brighter Days Ahead*, *Wicked: For Good* and What's Next?

1   https://deadline.com/2025/05/ariana-grande-meet-the-parents-movie-1236413786/

2   https://edition.cnn.com/2025/06/17/entertainment/ariana-grande-marjorie-nonna-death
3   https://edition.cnn.com/2025/06/17/entertainment/ariana-grande-marjorie-nonna-death
4   https://www.bbc.co.uk/news/entertainment-arts-68612693
5   https://www.tiktok.com/@varietymagazine/video/7446496199819136302
6   https://x.com/buzzingpop/status/1866945834010468579?s=46
7   https://www.hollywoodreporter.com/movies/movie-features/ariana-grande-wicked-oscars-music-love-1236132418/
8   https://www.screendaily.com/features/ariana-grande-on-her-wicked-journey-and-future-acting-projects-id-love-to-continue-on-this-road/5201532.article